Psychological Fitness and Resilience

A Review of Relevant Constructs, Measures, and Links to Well-Being

Sean Robson

RAND Project AIR FORCE

Prepared for the United States Air Force
Approved for public release; distribution unlimited

The research described in this report was sponsored by the United States Air Force under Contract FA7014-06-C-0001. Further information may be obtained from the Strategic Planning Division, Directorate of Plans, Hq USAF.

Library of Congress Control Number: 2014932040

ISBN: 978-0-8330-8076-9

Preface

U.S. military personnel have been engaged in operations in Central Asia and the Middle East for the past decade. Members of the armed forces also deploy to other regions of the world. Many aspects of deployments have the potential to contribute to individual stress, such as uncertainty about deployment time lines; culture shock in theater; fear of or confrontation with death or physical injury; environmental challenges, such as extreme climates and geographical features; austere living conditions; separation from friends and family members; and reintegration after deployment. Service members and their families also manage other military-related stressors, such as frequent relocations, long work hours, and the additional family separations associated with unaccompanied tours and domestic training exercises. Some service members and their families may cope well or even thrive as they overcome adversity and accomplish challenging tasks. However, some may suffer negative consequences as a result of military-related stressors, such as physical injury, including traumatic brain injury; depression, anxiety, or other mood disorders; post-traumatic stress disorder; spiritual crises; substance abuse; family dysfunction; marital problems and dissolutions; social isolation; and, in extreme cases, even suicide or suicide attempts. With the aim of preventing such deleterious outcomes rather than simply responding to them, the study of resilience is of paramount importance.

The Air Force offices of Airman and Family Services (AF/A1S), the Surgeon General (AF/SG), and the Secretary of the Air Force, Force Management and Personnel (SAF/MRM) asked the RAND Corporation to help the Air Force develop its programs to promote resiliency among military and civilian Air Force personnel and their families. This report is one in a series of nine reports that resulted from that research effort.

The overarching report, *Airman and Family Resilience: Lessons from the Scientific Literature* (Meadows and Miller, forthcoming), provides an introduction to resilience concepts and research, documents established and emerging Air Force resiliency efforts, and reviews Air Force metrics for tracking the resiliency of Air Force personnel and their families. It also provides recommendations to support the development of resilience initiatives across the Air Force. We use the term *resilience* to refer to the ability to withstand, recover from, and grow in the face of stressors and *fitness*, which is related, as a "state of adaptation in balance with the conditions at hand" (Mullen, 2010).

Accompanying that overarching report are eight supplemental reports that outline the constructs, metrics, and influential factors relevant to resiliency across the eight domains of Total Force Fitness:

- medical
- nutritional
- environmental
- physical
- social
- spiritual
- behavioral
- psychological.

These supplemental reports are not intended to be a comprehensive review of the entire literature within a domain. Rather, they focus on studies that consider the stress-buffering aspects of each domain, regardless of whether the term *resilience* is specifically used. This expanded the scope of the reviews to include a broader range of applicable studies and also allowed for terminology differences that occur across different disciplines (e.g., stress management, hardiness).

In this report, we identify key constructs relevant to psychological fitness from the scientific literature: self-regulation, positive affect, perceived control, self-efficacy, self-esteem, and optimism. This review includes construct measures as well as well-being and resilience outcomes. We also review interventions designed to promote those psychological fitness constructs.

The results of these reports should be relevant to Air Force leaders who are tasked with monitoring and supporting the well-being of active duty, reserve, and guard Airmen and Air force civilian employees, as well as their families. The results of our studies may also help broaden the scope of research on resilience and help Airmen and their families achieve optimal psychological fitness.

The research described in this report was conducted within the Manpower, Personnel, and Training Program of RAND Project AIR FORCE as part of a fiscal year 2011 study titled "Program and Facility Support for Air Force Personnel and Family Resiliency."

RAND Project AIR FORCE

RAND Project AIR FORCE (PAF), a division of the RAND Corporation, is the U.S. Air Force's federally funded research and development center for studies and analyses. PAF provides the Air Force with independent analyses of policy alternatives affecting the development, employment, combat readiness, and support of current and future air, space, and cyber forces. Research is conducted in four programs: Force Modernization and Employment; Manpower, Personnel, and Training; Resource Management; and Strategy and Doctrine.

Additional information about PAF is available on our website: http://www.rand.org/paf/

Contents

Summary

Psychological fitness, as part of the Total Force Fitness (TFF) construct, is defined as the integration and optimization of cognitive processes and abilities, behaviors, and emotions to positively affect performance, well-being, and response to stress. These resilience factors can be thought of as antecedents of a complex process whereby individuals deal with stress. As such, they provide the foundation for psychological fitness.

This report focuses on three categories of key resilience factors in the psychological domain: cognitive, affective, and self-regulatory. The cognitive category includes constructs that reflect individuals' thoughts and beliefs about themselves (e.g., self-efficacy, self-esteem), in addition to interpretations of their situation (e.g., perceived control). The affective category includes constructs that measure the experience of positive and negative emotions (e.g., positive and negative affect). And the self-regulatory category includes constructs that measure self-regulation and control (e.g., coping strategies). In general, the actual measurement of these psychological constructs is primarily accomplished via self-report survey or questionnaire.

The report also reviews existing research on training programs and interventions to promote the development of psychological fitness. Common themes across interventions to promote psychological fitness include two components: self-awareness and skill-building. Self-awareness is related to individuals' understanding of how they respond to stress, the emotions they experience, and their thought processes. Skill-building is associated with the promotion of positive emotions, happiness, confidence, self-esteem, and well-being.

It is important to bear in mind that much of the research conducted to date is correlational. Since correlation does not imply causation, it is difficult to draw strong conclusions about the potential benefits of interventions to promote resilience. Thus, interventions to promote psychological fitness may not be as effective as anticipated if other potential explanations for the correlation are not also examined.

Acknowledgments

This research was sponsored by the Air Force Resilience office and was led by Mr. Brian P. Borda for a significant portion of the study period and by Air Force Surgeon General Lt Gen (Dr.) Charles B. Green and Mr. William H. Booth, the Assistant Secretary of the Air Force for Manpower and Reserve Affairs (SAF/MRM).

We would like to thank the action officers from the sponsoring offices for their role in shaping the research agenda and providing feedback on interim and final briefings of the research findings. Those officers are Maj Kirby Bowling, our primary contact from the Air Force Resilience office; Col John Forbes and Lt Col David Dickey from the Air Force Surgeon General's office; and Linda Stephens-Jones from SAF/MRM. We also appreciate the insights and recommendations received from Ms. Eliza Nesmith while she was in the Air Force Services, and Lt Col Shawn Campbell while he served in the SAF/MRM office.

RAND's Sarah Meadows and Laura Miller led the overall research effort on resilience and provided extensive feedback on a previous draft of this manuscript. Donna White and Hosay Salam Yaqub provided valuable assistance formatting the manuscript and the bibliography for publication.

Finally, we would like to thank David Keyser, Grant Marshall, and Nicole Eberhart for taking the time and effort to review and provide guidance on ways to improve the overall quality of this report.

Abbreviations

CRM	crew resource management
DCoE	Defense Centers of Excellence
DoD	Department of Defense
EQ-I	Emotional Quotient Inventory
JAI	Job Adaptability Inventory
LOC	locus of control
LOT	Life Orientation Test
MBSR	mindfulness-based stress reduction
MRT	master resilience trainer
PANAS	Positive and Negative Affect Schedules
PSCS	private self-consciousness scale
PTSD	post-traumatic stress disorder
SOC	sense of coherence
SIT	stress inoculation training
TFF	Total Force Fitness

1. The Context of This Report[1]

This report is one of a series designed to support Air Force leaders in promoting resilience among Airmen, its civilian employees, and Air Force family members. The research sponsors requested that RAND assess the current resilience-related constructs and measures in the scientific literature and report any evidence of initiatives that promote resilience across a number of domains. We did not limit our search to research conducted in military settings or with military personnel, as Air Force leaders sought the potential opportunity to apply the results of these studies to a population that had not yet been addressed (i.e., Airmen). Further, many Air Force services support Air Force civilians and family members, and thus the results of civilian studies would apply to these populations.

This study adopts the Air Force definition of resilience: "the ability to withstand, recover and/or grow in the face of stressors and changing demands," which we found to encompass a range of definitions of resilience given throughout the scientific literature.[2] By focusing on resilience, the armed forces aim to expand their care to ensure the well-being of military personnel and their families through preventive measures and not just by treating members after they begin to experience negative outcomes (e.g., depression, anxiety, insomnia, substance abuse, post-traumatic stress disorder, or suicidal ideation).

Admiral Michael Mullen, Chairman of the Joint Chiefs of Staff from 2007 to 2011, outlined the concept of Total Force Fitness (TFF) in a special issue of the journal *Military Medicine*: "A total force that has achieved total fitness is healthy, ready, and resilient; capable of meeting challenges and surviving threats" (Mullen, 2010, p. 1). This notion of "fitness" is directly related to the concept of resilience. The same issue of *Military Medicine* also reflected the collective effort of scholars, health professionals, and military personnel, who outlined eight domains of TFF: medical, nutritional, environmental, physical, social, spiritual, behavioral, and psychological. This framework expands on the traditional conceptualization of resilience by looking beyond the psychological realm to also emphasize the mind-body connection and the interdependence of each of the eight domains.

The research sponsors requested that RAND adopt these eight fitness domains as the organizing framework for our literature review. We followed this general framework, although in some cases we adapted the scope of a domain to better reflect the relevant research. Thus, this study resulted in eight reports, each focusing on resilience-related research in one of the TFF

---

[1] Adapted from Meadows and Miller, forthcoming.

[2] The Air Force adopted this definition, which was developed by the Defense Centers of Excellence for Psychological Health and Traumatic Brain Injury (DCoE, 2011).

domains, but we note that not all of these domains are mutually exclusive. These eight reports define each domain and address the following interrelated topics:

- medical: preventive care, the presence and management of injuries, chronic conditions, and barriers and bridges to accessing appropriate quality health care (Shih, Meadows, and Martin, 2013)
- nutritional: food intake, dietary patterns and behavior, and the food environment (Flórez, Shih, and Martin, forthcoming)
- environmental: environmental stressors and potential workplace injuries and preventive and protective factors (Shih, Meadows, Mendeloff, and Bowling, forthcoming)
- physical: physical activity and fitness (Robson, 2013)
- social: social fitness and social support from family, friends, coworkers/unit members, neighbors, and cyber communities (McGene, 2013)
- spiritual: spiritual worldview, personal religious or spiritual practices and rituals, support from a spiritual community, and and spiritual coping (Yeung and Martin, 2013)
- behavioral: health behaviors related to sleep and to drug, alcohol, and tobacco use (Robson and Salcedo, forthcoming)
- psychological: self-regulation, positive and negative affect, perceived control, self-efficacy, self-esteem, optimism, adaptability, self-awareness, and emotional intelligence (Robson, 2014).

These reports are not intended to be comprehensive reviews of the entire literature within a domain. Rather, they focus on those studies that consider the stress-buffering aspects of each domain, regardless of whether the term *resilience* is specifically used. This expanded the scope of the reviews to include a broader range of studies and also allowed for differences in the terminology used across different disciplines (e.g., stress management, hardiness). We sought evidence both on the main effects of resilience factors in each domain (i.e., those that promote general well-being) and on the indirect or interactive effects (i.e., those that buffer the negative effects of stress).

Because the Air Force commissioned this research to specifically address individuals' capacity to be resilient, and thus their well-being, our reports do not address whether or how fitness in each of the eight TFF domains could be linked to other outcomes of interest to the military, such as performance, military discipline, unit readiness, personnel costs, attrition, or retention. Those worthy topics were beyond the scope of this project.

Some other important parameters shaped this literature review. First, across the study, we focused on research from the past decade, although older studies are included, particularly landmark studies that still define the research landscape or where a particular line of inquiry has been dormant in recent years. Second, we prioritized research on adults in the United States. Research on children was included where particularly germane (e.g., in discussions of family as a form of social support), and, occasionally, research on adults in other Western nations is referenced or subsumed within a large study. Research on elderly populations was generally excluded. Third, we prioritized literature reviews, meta-analyses, and on-going bodies of research over more singular smaller-scale studies.

The search for evidence on ways to promote resilience in each domain included both actions that individuals could take as well as actions that organizations could take, such as information campaigns, policies, directives, programs, initiatives, facilities, or other resources. We did not filter out evidence related to Air Force practices already under way, as the Air Force was interested both in research related to existing practices and in research that might suggest new paths for promoting resilience. Our aim was not to collect examples of creative or promising initiatives at large but to seek scholarly publications assessing the stress-buffering capacity of initiatives. Thus, in general, this collection of reviews does not address initiatives that have not yet been evaluated for their effect.

Building on the foundation of the eight reports that assess the scientific literature in each domain, RAND prepared an overarching report that brings together the highlights of these reviews and examines their relevance to current Air Force metrics and programs. That ninth report, *Airman and Family Resilience: Lessons from the Scientific Literature,* provides a more in-depth introduction to resilience concepts and research, presents our model of the relationship between resilience and TFF, documents established and emerging Air Force resiliency efforts, and reviews the Air Force metrics for tracking the resiliency of Air Force personnel and their families. By comparing the information we found in the research literature to Air Force practices, we were able to provide recommendations to support the development of initiatives to promote resilience across the Air Force. Although the overview report contains Air Force–specific recommendations that take into account all eight domains and existing Air Force practices, some are applicable to the military more generally and are highlighted at the end of this report.

2. Psychological Fitness Constructs and Measures

"People are not disturbed by things, but by the view they take of them."
— Epictetus, Philosopher

Research on psychological resilience has expanded considerably in recent years. This growth has resulted in many different definitions and models to describe the situational factors, individual traits, and internal and external resources that can facilitate resilience. The focus of these models can be characterized along a state-trait continuum. Models that focus on relatively stable factors, such as personality, intelligence, or core self-evaluations, are considered to be more trait-like, whereas state-like models emphasize malleable or changeable factors, such as an individual's moods, self-efficacy, or optimism (Luthans et al., 2007). Although trait models can enhance our theoretical understanding of resilience, state-like models can provide practical suggestions for enhancing resilience by focusing on resources that can be developed.

Building on the conservation of resources theory and the job demand-resource model, Bates et al. (2010) propose a military demand-resource model. This model suggests that resilience can be positively influenced by building internal and external resources to successfully respond to different demands (i.e., stressors). In contrast, other models suggest that resilience is a function of a person's individual traits and characteristics.

Although many definitions of psychological resilience have been offered, these are limited in several ways. First, some of these definitions focus on protective factors or the absence of specific negative outcomes, such as those that emphasize the prevention of mental disorders (Richardson, 2002). Although the prevention of mental disorders (e.g., depression) is clearly an important goal of many resilience programs, building the capacity to be resilient with an emphasis on growth and happiness has continued to emerge with a different perspective on resilience (Lyubomirsky and Della Porta, 2010). The goal is not simply to prevent an adverse psychological state but to pursue happiness, well-being, and high levels of performance. Second, other definitions focus primarily on individual characteristics and traits while providing limited attention to the processes used to appraise and cope with stress. Modifying the appraisal process or explanatory style of individuals is a major component of some intervention efforts to enhance resilience (Cornum, Matthews, and Seligman, 2011; Reivich, Seligman, and McBride, 2011; Seligman and Fowler, 2011).

Recognizing the goals of the military to enhance resilience by building resources and the skills to use those resources, a slightly modified version of the Bates et al. (2010) definition is provided to emphasize the development of internal and external resources to facilitate resilience. That is, psychological fitness is the integration and optimization of cognitive processes and abilities, behaviors, and emotions to positively impact performance, well-being, and response to stress. In other words, psychological fitness represents resources that, if available and used, can increase an individual's ability to respond to stressful events (i.e., resilience). Consistent with the Marine Corps publication on Combat Operational Stress, this definition promotes the identification and strengthening of resources to promote mental health. This perspective suggests that psychological fitness comprises resources that can increase or decrease over time. Maximizing these resources facilitates resilience, which is the ability to withstand, recover from, and/or grow in the face of stressors and changing demands.

Psychological resources have been the focus of theories of resilience, stress prevention, and overall psychological health and well-being. Although the focus and contributions of each theory are slightly different, several key psychological constructs emerge as important resources for strengthening resilience and resistance to stress.

Although background (e.g., childhood trauma, socioeconomic status) and psychological disorders including depression, anxiety, and post-traumatic stress disorder (PTSD) can be a sign of poor psychological resilience and may also make people more vulnerable to stress, these topics are not the primary focus of this report. Extensive research has been conducted on these topics with dedicated attention to understanding these problems in military populations and evidence-based interventions, in particular because of the wartime experiences of service members and concerns about the rates of PTSD and suicide (Hoge et al., 2004; Meredith et al., 2011; Ramchand et al., 2011; Tanielian et al., 2008). Indeed, a Defense Center of Excellence on Psychological Health and Traumatic Brain Injury[1] was established in 2007, and part of its mission is to focus on these issues by facilitating treatment programs, research, and outreach. However, resiliency efforts in the Department of Defense (DoD) and the Air Force emphasize the need to strengthen psychological health and well-being long before psychological disorders have begun to emerge. Therefore, the focus of this report is on the psychological resources that can promote resilience.

Several psychological resources were identified in the literature review, which generally fell into one of three broad domains: (1) self-regulatory, (2) affective, or (3) cognitive. The self-regulatory domain includes measures of self-regulation and strategies to cope with stress. The affective domain specifically refers to the experience of positive and negative emotions. This domain would include measures of both positive and negative affect. Finally, the cognitive domain includes measures reflecting individuals' thoughts, beliefs, and evaluations of themselves and their interpretations of their situation. An overview is provided of some additional psychological resources that relate to both the cognitive and self-regulatory domains (i.e., adaptability, self-awareness, and emotional intelligence), although these resources have not been as extensively studied in the context of resilience,

The following chapters of this report are organized into two main parts; in the first part, each construct is defined, followed by a review of research supporting the relevance to psychological

---

[1] http://www.dcoe.health.mil/.

fitness, and an overview of common approaches for measuring the construct. In the second part of this report, research is presented on training programs and interventions to promote the development of psychological fitness. As the supporting evidence for each resource is discussed, it is important to remember that much of the research conducted to date is correlational, making it difficult to determine the true nature of observed relationships. For example, optimism may lead to increased/decreased happiness, happiness may increase/decrease optimistic thinking, or there may be another variable (e.g., job promotion or loss) contributing to increases/decreases in both happiness and optimism.

3. Psychological Fitness Constructs and Measures

This chapter reviews prominent constructs within the psychological domain that have been linked to health, well-being, and resilience. They include self-regulation, positive and negative affect, perceived control, self-efficacy, self-esteem, and optimism. Multidimensional constructs relevant to psychological fitness were also included in the course of this review. However, these multidimensional constructs often contain dimensions that are more directly relevant to other TFF domains. For example, Ryff's (1989) structure of well-being includes *positive relations with others* as one of six core dimensions of well-being. Although relevant to psychological fitness, personal relationships are covered in detail in the companion report on social fitness (McGene, 2013). Other examples of multidimensional constructs that contain dimensions relevant to multiple TFF domains include hardiness (Bartone et al., 2008; Eschleman, Bowling, and Alarcon, 2010; Maddi, 2002, 2005, 2007; Skomorovsky and Sudom, 2011; Vogt et al., 2008) and sense of coherence (SOC) Antonovsky, 1984, 1993; Antonovsky and Sagy, 1986). Although these multidimensional constructs are not fully evaluated in this report, their relevant dimensions to psychological fitness are discussed within the context of the framework presented below. For example, hardiness is generally thought of as a composite of three factors: commitment, control, and challenge. Control and challenge are related to constructs discussed in this report (e.g., perceived control, coping). The first factor, commitment, is related to a sense of purpose, which is discussed in the companion report on spiritual fitness (Yeung and Martin, 2013).

Also included is a set of additional psychological resources that have seen less attention in the literature but have recently emerged as important for stress-buffering and overall psychological health. These include adaptability, self-awareness, and emotional intelligence. Where possible the chapter also notes how each construct has been measured.

For each construct, a definition is provided followed by an overview of research and common approaches for measuring each construct. To date, most measurement approaches have used self-reports to assess psychological constructs. More recent attempts to measure stress responses and psychological states have used physiological measures such as electroencephalogram, event related potentials, and heart rate variability. Although physiological measures may overcome some of the known limitations of self-report measures (e.g., self-enhancement bias), they are generally used in clinical applications, can be expensive, and are less practical for large populations. For these reasons, such physiological measures are not considered as part of this review.

Self-Regulation

Definition

An important building block for the development of many psychological resources, "[s]elf-regulation refers to those processes internal and/or transactional, that enable an individual to guide his/her goal-directed activities over time and across circumstances" (Karoly, 1993, p. 25). This ability affects the regulation of emotions, thought-processes, behaviors, and performance (Baumeister, Heatherton, and Tice, 1994).

Supporting Research

Early research suggested that three main components provide the foundation for self-regulation (Carver and Scheier, 1982): (a) having a clear set of standards, (b) monitoring one's current state to determine any deviation from set standards, and (c) an operate phase in which one attempts to modify the current state when a deviation from the set standard is identified (Baumeister and Heatherton, 1996). Using weight control as an illustrative example, one may determine that 175 lb is his standard for a healthy weight. After weighing himself, he recognizes that he is 10 lb heavier than his preferred weight. Finally, he changes his behavior, perhaps by modifying his diet or exercising more regularly, to bring his weight back to 175 lb.

More recent research has begun to uncover the neural basis for many important self-regulatory functions. For example, different areas of the prefrontal cortex in the brain appear to be particularly important to self-regulation (Heatherton, 2011). When these regions of the brain are damaged, individuals have been found to have difficulty in controlling their behavior, planning actions, and regulating goals, as well as to suffer from decreased motivation. These findings highlight the importance of both conscious and unconscious (i.e., neurological) processes in the regulation of emotions, thoughts, and behaviors. Indeed, it is now recognized that both types of processes work to control behavior (Posner and Rothbart, 2000).

Self-regulatory failure has been implicated in many societal problems where individuals fail to set standards, monitor their behavior, or change their behavior. For example, inability to delay gratification, procrastination, consumption of alcohol and tobacco, and other health-related behaviors have all been subject to analysis of failed self-regulation (Baumeister and Heatherton, 1996). Not only does self-regulation facilitate the ability to exercise restraint, direct choices, and persist in the face of adversity, but it is also important in helping individuals to "bounce back" after experiencing stress. For example, Aspinwall and Taylor (1997) argue that self-regulation can help individuals avoid or minimize stress through anticipation and proactive coping. Furthermore, recent theoretical advances in developmental epidemiology directly implicate poor self-regulation as a critical risk factor for the development of PTSD (Koenen, 2006). This theoretical framework suggests that self-regulation not only directly affects how individuals respond following a traumatic event but may also indirectly increase the risk of exposure to trauma. For example, those with poor self-regulation may be more likely to abuse drugs and alcohol, which heightens their risk of exposure to a serious car accident.

Measurement

Self-regulation has most frequently been measured in laboratory settings under carefully controlled conditions. Many of these measures objectively assess self-regulation by assessing the ability to delay gratification, persist on difficult or impossible tasks, or control attention processes. For example, the Stroop task[1] has been used to measure self-regulatory depletion under varying conditions (e.g., Richeson and Shelton, 2003). Other researchers have developed self-report measures of self-regulation (e.g., Brandon, Oescher, and Loftin, 1990; Rosenbaum, 1980). These measures can detect broad differences in self-regulation; however, considerable intra-individual changes in self-regulation occur over time. Consistent with neuroimaging studies showing decreased activity in certain regions of the brain (Heatherton, 2011), self-regulation can be viewed as a limited resource, which must be replenished following the exertion of self-control (Muraven and Baumeister, 2000). Consequently, self-report measures may be insensitive to measuring one's current capacity for self-regulation. Nonetheless, self-report measures have been used to predict academic grades, adjustment, alcohol abuse, and quality of relationships (Tangney, Baumeister, and Boone, 2004). A third method of measuring self-regulation involves observational ratings of behavior (Dembinski, 1979). Observational ratings provide several advantages over self-report measures including the elimination of self-report bias; however, they are more time-consuming to administer and require trained raters and a sampling design that captures representative behaviors.

Coping Strategies

Definition

Coping involves "the ways people actually respond to stress, such as through seeking help, rumination, problem solving, denial, or cognitive restructuring" (Skinner et al. , 2003, p. 216). A vast literature has been developed to identify the full range of coping strategies and to determine their effectiveness in handling stress. Much of this literature is based on the cognitive theories of stress and coping such as the Transactional Theory of Stress and Coping (Lazarus and Folkman, 1984). A major feature of this theory is that individuals make two types of decisions; first, they evaluate the relevance of the stressors to their lives (i.e., primary appraisal) and, second, they determine what can be done (i.e., secondary appraisal). This secondary appraisal occurs when a choice to use a particular coping strategy is made to deal with the stressor. For example, an

---

[1] The Stroop task provides a list of color words to participants and requires that they to name the ink color of the word. This is a challenging task because the color words (e.g., red) can be different from the ink color (e.g., blue).

11

individual who receives constant criticism from a supervisor may attempt to decrease this perceived stress by working harder or longer hours to please the supervisor.

The specific coping strategy selected by individuals is influenced by many factors, including their environmental factors as well as their predisposition to use a specific strategy. For example, research has shown that individuals who are extroverted and conscientious are more likely to use problem-solving and cognitive restructuring coping strategies. In contrast, individuals high in neuroticism are more likely to use wishful thinking and withdrawal strategies (Connor-Smith and Flachsbart, 2007). These predispositions or tendencies to use a specific type of coping strategy are often referred to as coping styles or dispositional coping. Since coping styles tend to be more stable and relate to the use of specific strategies, they may not result in effective coping in all situations. Research, discussed below, highlights the potential value in remaining flexible when selecting a particular coping strategy.

Efforts over the past few decades have yielded the development of at least 100 assessments of coping styles and over 400 labels, prompting some confusion about the major categories of coping (Skinner et al., 2003). Although research has begun to clarify the structure of these coping strategies (Skinner et al., 2003), the broad distinctions used by others (e.g., Compas et al., 2001) that differentiate between problem-focused and emotion-focused coping and between approach/engagement and avoidance/disengagement strategies[2] provide the foundation for the following overview of research on coping. These forms of coping reflect individual differences in anticipation and reaction to stress (Roth and Cohen, 1986). More specifically, high levels of attention to the stressor and the use of such strategies as gathering information, planning, and active problem-solving characterize approach/engagement strategies. In contrast, avoidance/disengagement reflect such strategies as inattention, withdrawal, and distraction.

Supporting Research

In general, research indicates that problem-focused coping is adaptive whereas emotion-focused coping is largely ineffective and even maladaptive in responding to stress demands (cf., Gilbar, Ben-Zur, and Lubin, 2010). Although meta-analyses, and a few select studies described below, highlight and provide some support for this finding, the current consensus is that no single coping strategy is effective or ineffective in all situations. Nonetheless, efforts continue to identify the boundary conditions and contexts in which different coping strategies are effective.

In separate studies on stress in the military, emotion-focused coping was found to predict stress symptoms during survival training (Taylor et al., 2009) and distress and poor performance among soldiers performing an evacuation task (Gilbar, Ben-Zur, and Lubin, 2010). Similar results from a group of fire-service personnel show that avoidance coping was associated with

---

[2] It should be noted that some researchers have argued that these broad categories oversimplify coping strategies (Carver, Scheier, and Weintraub, 1989), which may obscure important relationships between more specific coping strategies and mental health.

higher reports of PTSD symptoms (Beaton et al., 1999). Studies of Israeli soldiers reveal similar patterns, with fewer PTSD symptoms among those who used problem-focus coping strategies and more symptoms among those using emotion-focused coping (Solomon, Mikulincer, and Flum, 1988). Reviews of coping in children and adolescents have also concluded that problem-solving coping and engagement coping are generally associated with better psychological adjustment, whereas disengagement and emotion-focused strategies are mostly associated with poorer psychological adjustment (Compas et al., 2001). Avoidance coping was also found, in another meta-analysis, to relate to higher psychological distress, depression, and PTSD symptoms among individuals coping with traumatic events (Littleton et al., 2007).

However, not all studies have supported the detrimental effects of emotion-focused coping. For example, some research has found that the conceptualization and measurement of emotion-focused coping is often confounded and can lead to erroneous conclusions about any potential benefit of such coping strategies (Stanton et al., 1994). Furthermore, the type of stress (e.g., controllable versus uncontrollable) and the specific coping strategy used may be important factors affecting coping efficacy. In fact, the severity of combat exposure has been identified as a potentially important moderator of the relationship between emotion-focused coping and PTSD in national guard and reserve service members (Rodrigues and Renshaw, 2010). Specifically, emotion-focused coping was associated with higher levels of PTSD only when moderate levels of combat exposure were experienced. Furthermore, at very high levels of combat exposure, emotion-focused coping was associated with lower levels of PTSD. Other researchers criticizing the simple dichotomy between emotion and problem-focused coping have further discriminated among subtypes of emotion-focused coping. In one such study, Austenfeld and Stanton (2004) demonstrated that improved measures of emotion-focused coping, which capture acknowledging, understanding, and expressing emotion, are adaptive in certain contexts. Other distinctions among emotion-focused coping strategies have been made in an attempt to refine theoretical and empirical models specifying the coping-health relationship.

One particular type of emotion-regulation strategy—positive reappraisal—appears to be especially beneficial for dealing with stress. Cognitive reappraisal, more generally, involves changing the way that one views a situation to be more positive (John and Gross, 2004). More specifically, positive reappraisal is about looking on the bright side or finding the silver lining when in a stressful situation. In examining resilience to stress, research shows that positive reappraisal can be a useful strategy for coping with stress and has been associated with better psychological adjustment in children and adolescents (Compas et al., 2001). In reviewing a series of experimental and correlational studies, John and Gross (2004) provide support for positive reappraisal for both its short- and long-term benefits on emotion and psychological health. However, positive reappraisal may not be an important resource for all types of outcomes. In a meta-analysis on health outcomes, positive reappraisal was significantly related to psychological health but was not associated with physical health outcomes when coping with health-related stress (Penley, Tomaka, and Wiebe, 2002). Other coping strategies and the type of stress included in this study indicated that specific features related to the stressor and the type of health outcomes examined will affect the relative effectiveness of any particular coping strategy. This line of thinking is consistent with research encouraging the flexible application of coping (Cheng, 2001). That is, there are often multiple ways to cope effectively, and being flexible provides individuals with the resources necessary to adjust their strategy when responding to different stressors. In fact, recent research indicates that lower levels of coping flexibility are associated with greater levels of complicated grief for bereaved individuals (Burton et al., 2011).

It should be noted, however, that the relationship between coping and mental health is most likely bidirectional. That is, coping can directly affect mental health, but poor initial mental health contributes to the use of maladaptive coping strategies (Aldwin and Revenson, 1987).

Measurement

Coping strategies are generally assessed using self-report instruments. However, these assessments differ in their target population (e.g., children versus adults) and focus. For example, some scales attempt to measure coping for general stress and negative events, whereas others measure specific life domains (e.g., work) or such specific stressors as coping with cancer (Skinner et al., 2003). Although alternative options for assessing coping are available (e.g., interviews, observation), far fewer of these instruments have been developed and used.

Positive and Negative Affect

Definition

Affect generally refers to an individual's "subjective sense of positivity or negativity arising from an event" (Carver and Harmon-Jones, 2009, p. 183). In other words, affect reflects the feelings and emotions a person experiences in different situations. Positive affect is the extent that an individual "feels enthusiastic, active, and alert," whereas "negative affect is a general dimension of subjective distress and unpleasurable engagement that subsumes a variety of aversive mood states, including anger, contempt, disgust, guilt, fear, and nervousness" (Watson, Clark, and Tellegen, 1988, p. 1063). Although other models have been developed to categorize the different emotions (cf., Carver and Harmon-Jones, 2009), recent evidence from neuroscience suggests that different prefrontal regions of the brain are activated in the experience of positive and negative emotions (Cacioppo et al., 2007). Furthermore, individuals differ in their baseline levels of activation in these regions, suggesting a predisposition to experiencing positive or negative emotions.

Supporting Research

Although a large body of research has consistently demonstrated the adverse relations between negative affect and well-being, more recent research examining positive affect suggests that positive emotions can spark the generation of additional positive states, which enhance well-being (Fredrickson and Joiner, 2002). This upward spiral involves broadening attention, cognition, and problem-solving, which facilitates the coping process in stressful situations. Evidence for the benefits of positive affect, summarized in a recent review, suggest that positive affect is related to "confidence, optimism, and self-efficacy; likeability and positive construal of others; sociability, activity, and energy; prosocial behavior; immunity and physical well-being; effective coping with challenge and stress; and originality and flexibility" (Lyubomirsky, King, and Diener, 2005, p. 804). Other evidence indicates that individuals who demonstrate positive psychological and social functioning, termed flourishing (Keyes, 2002), have a mean ratio of positive to negative affect of 2.9 and higher (Fredrickson and Losada, 2005). Furthermore, it is expected that individuals above this threshold will also be resilient in the face of adversity. In stressful situations, people can experience a range of negative emotions including fear, anger, sadness, or disgust (Bovin and Marx, 2011). However, resilient individuals also draw on positive emotions when stressed to regulate emotions[3] and to find positive meaning in their personal problems (Tugade and Fredrickson, 2004). Furthermore, the sustainment of positive affect during tough times can be adaptive, serving as a buffer against depression, distress, and the physiological consequences of stress (Folkman and Moskowitz, 2000; Fredrickson et al., 2003). The overall positive findings for building on positive emotions was acknowledged in a recent review of potential interventions for active duty military personnel (Morgan and Bibb, 2011).

Measurement

Positive and negative affects are measured using self-report instruments. The most widely used of these instruments is the Positive and Negative Affect Schedules, simply referred to as the PANAS (Watson, Clark, and Tellegen, 1988). The PANAS includes two 10-item scales comprising 20 mood-related adjectives.

Perceived Control

Definition

Perceived control can be defined by the extent to which people feel a sense of control over events (i.e., locus of control [LOC]) as well as being the initiator of their own behavior. Other terms used to reflect perceived control include autonomy and self-mastery (Pearlin and Schooler, 1978). Rotter (1966) distinguishes between an internal LOC and an external LOC. Those with an internal LOC believe that they have control over the events in their lives, whereas, those with an external attribution believe that events are caused by others, chance, or fate.

---

[3] Emotional intelligence may be an important ability in regulating emotions when under stress. It is discussed more in a later section on emerging constructs.

Supporting Research

LOC has been linked to a wide range of outcomes, largely indicating that an internal LOC is associated with positive benefits. For example, those with an internal LOC might believe that their performance evaluation scores were due to their own efforts. In contrast, individuals with an external LOC might believe that their performance evaluation scores were due to luck or to their assignment to a particular unit or supervisor, resulting in low expectations that increased efforts will lead to higher performance evaluation scores.

In two separate meta-analyses, an internal LOC was associated with several positive work outcomes, including positive task and social experiences and higher levels of motivation, satisfaction, and performance (Judge and Bono, 2001; Ng, Sorensen, and Eby, 2006). Other studies point to the risks of an external LOC, which include higher risk for depression and anxiety (Benassi, Sweeney, and Dufour, 1988; Johnson and Sarason, 1978). Furthermore, those with an external LOC tend to respond poorly to stress (Krause and Stryker, 1984) and demonstrate less happiness (Larson, 1989). Loss of perceived control has been shown to mediate the relationship between uncontrollable stress and substance abuse in adolescents (Newcomb and Harlow, 1986). In other words, uncontrollable stress is associated with reduced perceived control, which is ultimately related to increases in the risk for substance use.

LOC has also been linked to important outcomes in military populations. In a cross-sectional study examining PTSD, soldiers from the Lebanon war (1982) with less intense PTSD symptoms reported a more internal LOC, in addition to more perceived social support (Solomon, Mikulincer, and Avitzur, 1988). Longitudinal studies have also supported the importance of perceived control. In a study of perceived stress following a natural disaster, those individuals with an internal LOC perceived less stress and engaged in more task-focused coping behaviors (Anderson, 1977).

In addition to feeling a sense of control over events that occur in life, individuals also benefit from feeling a sense of control over their own behavior as opposed to being controlled and directed by others. Autonomy is a central component of theories of emotional well-being, and differences in perceived autonomy have been linked to both daily fluctuations in emotional well-being and to stable individual differences in well-being across people (Deci and Ryan, 1987; Reis et al., 2000). Furthermore, research shows that specific events and contexts, which support autonomy, are associated with a range of positive psychological states, including "more intrinsic motivation, greater interest, less pressure and tension, more creativity, more cognitive flexibility, better conceptual learning, a more positive emotional tone, higher self-esteem, more trust, greater persistence of behavior change, and better physical and psychology health" (Deci and Ryan, 1987, p. 1024).

Although a large body of research suggests that an internal LOC results in positive outcomes, there are risks when an individual with an internal LOC experiences negative events that are perceived to be stable. These attributional styles are discussed in the section on "Optimism," below. To briefly summarize, research generally shows that an internal LOC and greater autonomy are associated with positive benefits, whereas an external LOC is associated with risks for a variety of adverse outcomes.

Measurement

LOC is measured using self-report instruments, with the original Rotter I-E scale being the most popular. Other scales have been developed to focus on specific contexts, including dental, general health, mental health, and work (Beck, 1980; Spector, 1988; Winefield, 1982; Wood and Letak, 1982).

Self-Efficacy

Definition

Another construct related to self-regulation and control is perceived self-efficacy, which is "concerned with judgments of how well one can execute courses of action required to deal with prospective situations" (Bandura, 1982, p. 122). In other words, self-efficacy is the belief an individual can do something. These judgments, which influence choices and determine effort, are critical factors in how one might respond to a stressful situation. Specifically, those individuals low in perceived self-efficacy focus on their own deficiencies rather than on ways to succeed, which detracts attention from how to effectively respond to a stressful situation.

Supporting Research

Meta-analyses have shown that self-efficacy is positively associated with job performance and satisfaction (Judge and Bono, 2001; Stajkovic and Luthans, 1998) and academic performance and persistence (Multon, Brown, and Lent, 1991). More directly related to stress, self-efficacy has been incorporated into models of resilience (Rutter, 1985), which has been supported by subsequent research showing that individuals higher in self-efficacy experience less stress and autonomic arousal when attempting to solve challenging problems (Bandura et al., 1988). There is also evidence that perceived inefficacy induces stress, which may result in a poorly functioning immune system, whereas, the process of building efficacy to cope with a stressor enhances the immune system (Wiedenfeld et al., 1990). Perceived self-efficacy may also be an important resource when adapting or adjusting to change (Callan, Terry, and Schweitzer, 1994; Jones, 1986).

Measurement

Measuring self-efficacy is accomplished using self-report measures. Although some researchers have advocated for a generalized self-efficacy measure, many other researchers argue that self-efficacy is domain-specific. One might have high self-efficacy for school yet have relatively low efficacy for sports. Because of the domain-specificity of self-efficacy, many measures have been developed and validated. To encourage valid assessments of self-efficacy, Bandura (2006) outlined several important features of self-efficacy scales. For example, scale items should use "can do" versus "will do," should focus on behaviors or tasks that people can control, and should represent varying levels of difficulty for performing.

Self-Esteem

Definition

Self-esteem, concerned with the global evaluation of one's self-worth, is an important marker for overall well-being and represents one of Maslow's higher-order needs (Maslow, 1943).

Supporting Research

Research has repeatedly shown that overall life satisfaction and subjective well-being is strongly correlated with satisfaction with self or self-esteem (cf., Diener, 2009). Self-esteem is also an important predictor of burnout (Alarcon, Eschleman, and Bowling, 2009). The importance of self-esteem has been further developed in two prominent theories: terror management theory (Pyszczynski et al. , 2004) and sociometer theory (Leary et al., 1995).

Terror management theory suggests that people pursue positive self-evaluations to protect themselves from anxiety related to feelings of threat, vulnerability, and an awareness of one's mortality. Evidence supporting terror management theory is provided by studies showing that self-esteem buffers against this anxiety (Greenberg et al., 1992). Sociometer theory, on the other hand, emphasizes that self-esteem is an important indicator that an individual is accepted by other people. Thus, self-esteem may, in part, reflect the nature of one's social relationships. Indeed, people with low self-esteem tend to report more negative interactions with others (Lakey, Tardiff, and Drew, 1994).

There are considerable individual differences in self-esteem, with males having slightly higher self-esteem than females (Kling et al., 1999). Although generally considered a stable trait, a person's evaluation of his or her overall worth or self-esteem may change in response to certain threats. Threats to self-image and self-adequacy occur regularly in everyday life. Such threats may involve receiving negative feedback about one's job, parenting style, body shape, or personal choices. However, most people demonstrate resilience by maintaining a positive self-image in the face of threats through a process of rationalization and self-justification (Steele, Spencer, and Lynch, 1993).

In a review of the benefits of self-esteem, Baumeister et al. (2003) conclude that self-esteem supports happiness and resilience but that the data are not sufficient to justify development of efforts simply to raise self-esteem. Not only is there a lack of evidence for developing such programs, but there may also be certain risks to such enhancements, as certain categories of high self-esteem (e.g., narcissism) can lead to a variety of such negative outcomes as increased bullying, aggressive retaliatory behavior, and prejudice. Despite these concerns, self-esteem is a strong indicator of well-being and may be used as one of several metrics in assessing psychological fitness.

Measurement

Self-esteem is assessed using self-report instruments. The most widely used instrument is the Rosenberg Self-Esteem Scale (Rosenberg, 1965), which consists of 10 items (e.g., On the whole, I am satisfied with myself) on a scale ranging from strongly disagree to strongly agree. The scale has been used in numerous studies and has received empirical support for both validity and reliability. Other versions assessing self-esteem, including a one-item scale (Robins, Hendin, and Trzesniewski, 2001), have been developed and validated.

Optimism

Definition

Dispositional optimism has been defined as the "generalized expectancy for positive outcomes" (Prati and Pietrantoni, 2009, p. 365). That is, optimists have a positive outlook on life and generally expect positive outcomes (Scheier and Carver, 1985). Because of the strong relationships with many health and psychology constructs, optimism has been strongly implicated in models of resilience (Connor and Davidson, 2003; Haglund et al., 2007; Johnson et al., 2011; Youssef and Luthans, 2007).

Supporting Research

In a recent meta-analysis, optimism was found to be significantly correlated with physical health outcomes (Rasmussen, Scheier, and Greenhouse, 2009). Furthermore, optimism significantly predicted both subjective and objective measures of physical health; however, it was more strongly correlated with subjective measures. Research also shows that these positive health benefits occur even when beliefs about the future are unrealistically optimistic (Taylor et al., 2000). In fact, such beliefs may be particularly important resources for protecting mental health during and following distressing events.

Research has shown very clear benefits of optimism on psychological health and well-being. In particular, research shows a very strong relationship to happiness (Baumeister et al., 2003). Additionally, in two separate meta-analyses, optimism was found to be a moderately important predictor of post-traumatic growth (Prati and Pietrantoni, 2009), increased use of approach coping strategies, and reduced use of avoidance coping strategies (Nes and Segerstrom, 2006). Coping strategies will be discussed in more detail in the next section.

Using a slightly different framework, Seligman (2002) incorporates optimism as part of an individual's explanatory style. A person's explanatory or attributional style describes how that person explains successes and failures in life. In addition to the internality/externality dimension discussed above with locus of control, explanatory styles also include the extent to which a person explains outcomes as caused by stable factors (e.g., low ability) or unstable factors (e.g., poor preparation) and whether the effects are specific to a situation (e.g., relationship with supervisor) or more global (e.g., relationship with authority). In general, the optimists are those who use internal, stable, and global causes to explain their successes. When optimists experience a failure or setback, they tend to believe that the events causing failure were specific to the situation and can change. Consequently, optimists still believe that success is possible.

At the other end of the continuum, pessimists are more likely to use internal, stable, and global causes to explain similar negative events. For example, a pessimist might think, "I'm just not smart enough" after failing a certification test. These internal, stable, and global explanations for bad events broadly affect an individual's feelings of helplessness (Peterson, 1991). Indeed, a meta-analysis has shown that this negative explanatory style is a very good predictor of depression (Sweeney, Anderson, and Bailey, 1986). Additional strong evidence has also been provided by a longitudinal study of men showing that internal, stable, and global explanations for bad events at age 25 were related to overall health in later life (Peterson, Seligman, and Vaillant, 1988). Furthermore, explanatory style predicted health from ages 45-60, even when controlling for initial physical and mental health. One possible explanation for the effects of explanatory style on health is provided by the diathesis-stress hypothesis. This model suggests that the risk of illness increases when people with a pessimistic explanatory style experience stress. Support for this model demonstrating an interaction between explanatory style and stress was provided in a longitudinal study showing that illness increased as stress increased for those with a pessimistic style but not for those with an optimistic explanatory style (Jackson, Sellers, and Peterson, 2002).

It should be noted that optimism may also present certain drawbacks and risks. For example, high levels of optimism may be maladaptive when facing persistent stressors. More specifically, optimism has been shown to negatively affect immune functioning when one is faced with persistent or uncontrollable stressors (Cohen et al., 1999; Sieber et al., 1992). One plausible explanation for these seemingly contradictory findings is that optimists continue to remain engaged and problem-solve even when the outcome cannot be controlled (Segerstrom, 2005). These results suggest that optimism may increase risks to health when certain types of stressors are faced. Nonetheless, the clear majority of research shows that optimism produce positive effects and pessimism yields negative outcomes.

Measurement

Optimism is measured using self-report instruments. The most widely used scale is the Life Orientation Test (LOT), which measures positive and negative life expectancies (Scheier and Carver, 1985). To further clarify the dimensionality of optimism and pessimism, Chang,

Maydeu-Olivares, and D'Zurilla (1997) integrated items from the LOT with the Optimism and Pessimism Scale (Dember and Brooks, 1989; Dember et al., 1989) to produce the Extended Life Orientation Test, which has also received empirical support. A person's explanatory style can also be measured using self-report instruments. The Attributional Style Questionnaire (Peterson et al., 1982), which presents a series of hypothetical events and asks participants to determine the cause, is perhaps the most widely used instrument.

Additional Psychological Resources—Emerging Constructs

Adaptability

Definition

Closely related to constructs of coping, adaptability involves how an individual or team adjusts in response to novel or changing environments. Adaptability is a broad resource, which can aid not only in responding to stress but also in adjusting to new life roles (e.g., parenting, marriage), work roles (e.g., promotion, deployment), and evolving job demands (e.g., technology, new supervisor). Because life in general can be unpredictable, adaptability is a particularly important skill to develop. Building adaptability may also function to support the development of other more specific resilience resources.

Supporting Research

Although few explicit links to resilience have been made, adaptability has been studied in a variety of related contexts, such as decisionmaking (LePine, Colquitt, and Erez, 2000), individual performance (Chen, Thomas, and Wallace, 2005), and team performance (Rosen et al., 2011).

Despite having intuitive importance, adaptability and related constructs have not yet been clearly defined and measured. Until such issues have been addressed, efforts to promote and teach these skills can be difficult (Pulakos et al., 2000).

Measurement

Some measures such as the EQ-I (Emotional Quotient Inventory) (Bar-On, 2004) contain specific subscales for adaptability in their self-report measures. In an attempt to directly measure adaptability as a broad psychological construct, Pulakos et al. (2000) identified eight adaptive performance dimensions: (1) handling emergencies, (2) handling work stress, (3) solving problems creatively, (4) dealing with uncertain situations, (5) learning, (6) interpersonal adaptability, (7) cultural adaptability, and (8) physically oriented adaptability. Using military populations in part, these efforts led to the development and validation of the Job Adaptability Inventory (JAI).[4]

Self-Awareness

Definition

Military personnel often refer to self-awareness, or the historical maxim, "Know Thyself" proffered by Plato and Socrates, simply as the "Gut Check." Several other constructs related to self-awareness include self-knowledge, self-monitoring, introspection, meta-cognition, and meta-perception. Self-awareness may be one of several characteristics of emotional intelligence. In fact, the EQ-I refers to self-awareness as one core component of important intrapersonal skills.

Supporting Research

Self-awareness is also an important element of negative feedback models (Scheier and Carver, 1985). At a basic level, these models suggest that individuals first recognize that a discrepancy exists between actual and desired states. Following awareness of this discrepancy, goal-directed activity is triggered to restore homeostasis. For example, a supervisor responding to a crisis may recognize increasing difficulty in concentrating on key tasks. This recognition may trigger a number of coping strategies such as taking a deep breath, prioritizing tasks, and delegating appropriate tasks to team members.

Hippe (2004) further argues that self-awareness of one's strengths and weaknesses is a precursor to building resilience. Taking a similar position, Locke (2005) asserts that self-monitoring through introspection is a process important to both self-esteem and mental health. These arguments have been supported empirically by showing that self-awareness is a critical protective factor for anxiety and depression (Morrison and Cosden, 1997).

Measurement

Self-awareness and related constructs are typically assessed using self-report methods. Some of these scales, such as the private self-consciousness scale (PSCS) (Fenigstein, Scheier, and Buss, 1975), have been validated and used extensively in a variety of contexts. However, as noted by Trapnell and Campbell (1999), the PSCS has received considerable criticism, often regarding its underlying factor structure. Additional concerns reflect the direction of relationships between the PSCS and psychological distress. Specifically, higher scores on PSCS, which indicate higher levels of self-awareness, have been related to more psychological distress, not better psychological well-being. This apparent paradox resulted in the distinction between two types of self-awareness: (1) reflection, which involves "self-attentiveness motivated by curiosity . . . in the self" and (2) rumination, which involves "self-attentiveness motivated by perceived threats, losses, or injustices to the self" (Trapnell and Campbell, 1999, p. 297). This

---

[4] The JAI is a proprietary instrument of Personnel Decisions Research Institute.

distinction is an important one when encouraging self-awareness, as rumination may be more maladaptive, whereas reflection promotes psychological adjustment.

Mindfulness

Definition

A closely related concept to self-awareness, self-regulation, and emotional intelligence, mindfulness has gained considerable traction within the military. Mindfulness "is most commonly defined as the state of being attentive to and aware of what is taking place in the present" (Brown and Ryan, 2003, p. 822) and can be considered an important element of both psychological and spiritual fitness (Bates et al., 2010; Hufford, Fritts, and Rhodes, 2010). Mindfulness is derived from Buddhist meditation and aims to cultivate awareness and attention of the present moment (Kabat-Zinn, 2003). Additionally, it is believed the mindfulness can promote self-regulation and help individuals avoid engaging in automatic behaviors and thoughts, which may be maladaptive (Brown and Ryan, 2003).

Supporting Research

Although much of the research on mindfulness is focused on clinical applications, emerging research is identifying the potential role of mindfulness in aiding decisionmaking. For example, research has shown that mindfulness may have a significant role in adaptive decisionmaking for individuals who take risks (Lakey et al., 2007). Specifically, individuals with higher levels of mindfulness may be less overconfident when taking risks. Research has also shown that mindfulness is related to well-being, and interventions to increase mindfulness can reduce mood disturbance and stress in cancer patients (Brown and Ryan, 2003). One particular intervention—mindfulness-based stress reduction (MBSR)—includes teaching formal meditation techniques with an emphasis on daily practice. This intervention was originally designed to target individuals with physical and psychological problems but has more recently been expanded to healthy adults experiencing stress (Brown, Ryan, and Creswell, 2007). MBSR has received empirical support from a meta-analysis showing moderate improvement in both physical and mental health among a diverse group of participants (Grossman et al., 2004). Other studies on MBSR are presented in the next chapter.

Measurement

Mindfulness is measured using self-report scales, with the Mindful Attention Awareness Scale (Brown and Ryan, 2003) and the Freiburg Mindfulness Inventory (Walach et al., 2006) being two of the more common measures.

Emotional Intelligence

Despite the broad appeal of the term emotional intelligence, considerable controversy remains over the concept, definitions, and measurement (e.g., Locke, 2005). Two types of measurement approaches have been developed to assess emotional intelligence. The first approach adopts the perspective that emotional intelligence is an ability. That is, emotional intelligence is "the ability to monitor one's own and others' feelings and emotions, to discriminate among them and to use this information to guide one's thinking and actions" (Salovey and Mayer, 1990, p. 189). The second perspective, termed the trait approach, argues that emotional intelligence is reflected in specific patterns of personality, such as adaptability, self-awareness, and stress management. Although the construct validity of the trait approach has been heavily criticized (Mayer, Salovey, and Caruso, 2008), two separate meta-analyses indicate that the trait approach yields stronger relationships with health criteria, including physical and mental health (Martins, Ramalho, and Morin, 2010; Schutte et al., 2007).

Summary

This chapter reviewed psychological constructs related to overall health, well-being, and resilience. These constructs constitute antecedents or factors that provide the foundation for psychological fitness. In general these factors cluster in three domains: cognitive, affective, and self-regulatory. Cognitive factors include self-efficacy self-esteem, which reflect an individual's thoughts about his or her abilities. Cognitive factors also include the ways in which people view or interpret the situations in their lives (e.g., optimism, perceived control). Such constructs as positive and negative affect measure an individual's experience of positive emotions. Self-regulation and control are often reflected in an individual's coping strategy. Measurement of all of these psychological constructs tends to occur via self-report survey or questionnaire. In the next chapter, specific interventions to promote psychological fitness through these constructs are discussed.

4. Interventions to Promote Psychological Fitness

This chapter provides an overview of interventions available to promote psychological health and well-being that have been evaluated in systematic reviews and meta-analyses. Furthermore, the interventions examined are limited to studies focusing specifically on adult populations. In general, well-designed educational, psychological, and behavioral interventions have been shown to be effective in producing the desired outcomes (Lipsey and Wilson, 1993). As in the medical field, however, most efforts have been devoted to the design of interventions to treat disorders and illness rather than to promote health and well-being. Despite relatively less attention, some effective psychological interventions have been designed to target the appraisal, management, and response to stress (Brunwasser, Gillham, and Kim, 2009),[1] whereas others promote the development of more specific psychological resources, such as the experience of positive emotions (e.g., happiness, gratitude).

Although meta-analyses generally provide support for many of the interventions reviewed, programs must be designed explicitly with intended effect for specific populations. As stated by Durlak and Wells (1997), there is no single best approach for promoting psychological fitness. Additionally, the effectiveness of interventions will vary depending on the target population, the type of intervention, its specificity , and its overall purpose or.

The following sections review two broad perspectives for promoting resilience: (1) stress management strategies, which provides training on how to reduce or respond to stress, and (2) psychological skill training, which promotes the development of broad psychological resources to strengthen psychological fitness.

Stress Management Strategies

In this first section, a overview of strategies that have been designed to specifically prepare individuals to meet the challenges of working in stressful environments is provided. Three broad strategies were identified by Orasanu and Backer (1996) for potential adoption in military settings. The first strategy, stress training or stress management, is designed to provide individuals with the skills to reduce or modify the stress itself. Among the various stress reduction programs, stress inoculation training (SIT) (Meichenbaum, 1985) has received considerable attention and support. Designed for use primarily in clinical settings, SIT emphasizes seven objectives (p. 22):

1. Teach clients the transactional nature of stress and coping.

---

[1] The Penn Resiliency Program and hardiness training, two specific interventions designed to promote resilience, are discussed in the overarching report in this series (Meadows and Miller, forthcoming).

2. Train clients to self-monitor maladaptive thoughts, images, feelings and behaviors in order to facilitate adaptive appraisals.
3. Train clients in problem solving, that is, problem definition, consequence, anticipation, decision making, and feedback evaluation.
4. Model and rehearse direct-action, emotion-regulation, and self-control coping skills.
5. Teach clients how to use maladaptive responses as cues to implement their coping repertoires.
6. Offer practice in in vitro imaginal and in behavioral rehearsal and in vivo graded assignments that become increasingly demanding, to nurture clients' confidence in and utilization of their coping repertoires.
7. Help clients acquire sufficient knowledge, self-understanding, and coping skills to facilitate better ways of handling (un)expected stress situations.

To accomplish these objectives, SIT uses three distinct stages. The first stage, the conceptualization phase, emphasizes the ways in which stress relates to emotions and performance. This provides the clients with the opportunity to further understand and recognize how stress is affecting him or her. The second stage, skills acquisition and rehearsal, is focused on developing effective strategies for managing stress and methods for eliminating potential barriers to their implementation. The final stage, application and follow-through, provides clients with the opportunity to practice their new skills and strategies, first by rehearsing and practicing in the clinic and then gradually through exposure to real life stressors.

Some evidence demonstrating the effectiveness of SIT was provided in a meta-analysis of 37 studies (Saunders et al., 1996). The findings indicated that SIT has moderate effects on the reductions of both performance and state anxiety and increased performance in stressful conditions. Although some evidence indicated that the effectiveness of SIT increases with increasing number of sessions, four to seven sessions were found to achieve average effects, with even a single session showing some benefits.

A more recent meta-analysis examined several types of occupational stress management interventions, including cognitive-behavioral (e.g., reframing stressful situations, stress inoculation training), relaxation (e.g., meditation, deep-breathing), organizational (e.g., goal-setting, coworker support group), multimodal, and alternative (e.g., journal writing, stress education) (Richardson and Rothstein, 2008). The results indicated that interventions with cognitive-behavioral treatment components had consistently stronger effects overall, specifically producing strong effects on mental health and anxiety.

The second strategy identified by Orasanu and Backer (1996) is skill training. The goal of this strategy is to develop durable job skills and expertise to the point where performance levels are maintained under a variety of stressful conditions. For example, overlearning or the continuation of skill training past mastery has been shown to have positive effects on retention (Driskell, Willis, and Copper, 1992). The additional confidence and perceived control from overlearning may also help to reduce the levels of stress experienced.

The final strategy discussed by Orasanu and Backer (1996) is crew resource management (CRM) training. Although developed to aid in cockpit management, the elements of this training can be effectively applied to other contexts in which teams must coordinate, communicate, manage resources, and make decisions while experiencing different stressors (e.g., time pressure, information overload, environmental hazards). One goal of CRM is to enhance the communication and coordination of crew teams to ensure the use of available information, personnel, and equipment (Salas et al., 2001). Support for the effectiveness of CRM was provided in two separate meta-analyses (O' Connor et al., 2008; Salas et al., 2001). These studies indicated that CRM had moderate to strong effects on trainee reactions, learning, and behavioral change.

Psychological Skill Training

Attention is now shifted to focus on interventions designed to enhance specific psychological skills that provide a foundation for resilience. That is, interventions have been developed to promote positive emotions and psychological well-being, self-efficacy, and self-regulation.

The recent emphasis on positive psychology and learned optimism focuses on promoting psychological well-being with specific exercises that enhance positive emotions and reframe one's cognitive perspective (Seligman, 2011a). Examples of these interventions, recently reviewed in a meta-analytic study of 51 interventions (Sin and Lyubomirsky, 2009), include savoring the moment by taking time to enjoy daily activities, emphasizing or using personal strengths in new ways, and keeping track of positive experiences (Seligman, Rashid, and Parks, 2006; Seligman et al., 2005). The results demonstrated overall moderate effects for enhancing well-being and decreasing depressive symptoms; however, variability was noted across several factors. Specifically, individuals who self-selected and were more depressed initially were found to experience greater gains from these interventions. Furthermore, the effects were strongest for individual therapy with progressively weaker effects for group-based and self-administered interventions. In general, though, reviews of research on programs to boost happiness have shown that happiness-enhancing strategies are generally effective for a wide range of people (Lyubomirsky and Della Porta, 2010).

Interventions to enhance self-efficacy have also been attempted. Self-efficacy interventions are based on different sources of information that individuals use to form beliefs about their capabilities and probability of success. These sources "include a) direct mastery experiences, b) observing people similar to oneself success by perseverant effort, c) social persuasion that one possesses the capabilities to succeed, and d) judgments of bodily states and various forms of somatic information" (Bandura, 1989, pp. 733-734). Common interventions to enhance self-efficacy focus on problem-solving, building confidence, skill mastery, and autonomy in decisionmaking. In a review of such interventions specifically designed for reducing chronic disability, Marks et al. (2005) found that successful interventions contained several features,

27

such as the inclusion of significant others, promotion of self-management, encouragement and support, and the fostering of self-appraisal of emotional and physiological responses.

Similar to self-efficacy interventions for chronic disease, other attempts have been made to develop interventions to promote self-regulation for physical health (Maes and Karoly, 2005); however, few of these interventions have been replicated. One category of interventions that has received extensive support for enhancing the regulation of behavior is goal-setting. Goal-setting can help promote desired behavior changes (e.g., physical activity) and improve performance (Locke, 1996; Locke and Latham, 2002; Shilts, Horowitz, and Townsend, 2004). In particular, goal-setting promotes self-regulation by directing action, increasing effort, and encouraging persistence until goals have been met. Effective goals share several features; they are challenging, specific, and personally relevant and can be objectively measured so that individuals can monitor their progress. When setting particularly challenging goals, it is important to ensure that the individual has the requisite skills and confidence (i.e., self-efficacy); otherwise, effort and commitment toward achieving the goal will be adversely affected.

Other types of skills training have focused on alternative modalities, such as yoga and meditation (e.g., Harinath et al., 2004). Few systematic reviews have been conducted on these methods; however, a recent meta-analysis on a limited number of studies showed that mindfulness based stress reduction (i.e., meditation) can reduce stress (Chiesa and Serretti, 2009). Similarly, few systematic reviews or controlled studies been conducted on programs designed to promote resilience in the military (Morgan and Bibb, 2011). For example, the Comprehensive Solder Fitness program was recently implemented to increase resilience across the entire U.S. Army (Casey, 2011; Cornum, Matthews, and Seligman, 2011; Seligman and Fowler, 2011). This program uses non-commissioned officers who are trained to be master resilence trainers (MRTs). The MRT's role is to provide resilience training to other soldiers within the units. Although evidence-based research was used to design the program, additional research is needed to determine its effectiveness for promoting resilience across the Army.

Mindfulness-Based Stress Reduction

MBSR is a group-based intervention designed to promote awareness in the present moment. This includes raising awareness of one's immediate feelings (e.g., physical sensations, mood) and thoughts. The primary objective of this intervention is to increase an individual's attention while withholding any evaluation of those thoughts or feelings. This increased attention allows individuals to more easily determine the accuracy of their thoughts and emotions. Although MBSR typically requires participation in eight sessions, each lasting 2.5 hours, followed by an intensive six-hour final session, some research evidence suggests that shorter interventions may still be effective in reducing psychological distress (Carmody and Baer, 2009).

Meta-analyses on MBSR have shown to improve physical and mental well-being (Chiesa and Serretti, 2009; Grossman et al., 2004). More recent research has also resulted in positive findings. For example, mindfulness training was shown to improve working memory capacity in military personnel who were preparing for deployment (Jha et al., 2010). However, it is important to note that these positive results were found only among personnel who engaged in considerable practice. Those personnel in a low practice condition actually experienced a decrease in working memory capacity. Despite the promising findings, both meta-analyses identified lack of quality in primary studies as a significant limitation. For example, of the 150 studies considered by Chiesa et al., only 10 met the criteria for inclusion. Additional research is needed to determine how well MBSR works in different populations who may experience very different stressors.

Summary

Overall, research suggests that interventions to promote psychological fitness may be beneficial. However, additional research needs to be conducted to evaluate how effective these strategies are with different populations and within the Air Force. Consequently, an optimal approach to building psychological resources may require a level of specificity in identifying the needs of subpopulations within the Air Force and the types of stressors commonly experienced. In addition, the timing of the intervention may also be an important factor to consider during implementation. Specifically, the Air Force may want to ensure that airmen have the psychological resources before they experience critical transitions such as deployments, returning from deployments, and duty relocations.

5. Conclusion

This report has reviewed psychological fitness constructs related to overall health and well-being, as well as resilience and stress buffering. Following a thorough review of the scientific literature, the antecedents of psychological health, or those factors and resources that provide a base for psychological fitness, were identified. These constructs cluster into three areas: cognitive, affective, and self-regulation.

Among the most important psychological constructs for psychological fitness are self-regulation and coping strategies, positive and negative affect, perceived control, self-efficacy, self-esteem, and optimism. All have received much attention in the existing literature; however, some emerging psychological fitness constructs have seen increased attention and appear to be linked to health and stress-buffering. These include adaptability, self-awareness, and emotional intelligence. Most of these constructs can be measured by using self-report questionnaire or survey data in the form of established scales.

Two broad types of intervention strategies—stress management and psychological skills training—were also reviewed. Available evidence for these strategies is positive, however, additional research needs to be conducted to evaluate how well these strategies work for the Air Force.

References

Alarcon, G., Eschleman, K., and Bowling, N. (2009). Relationships between personality variables and burnout: A meta-analysis. *Work & Stress, 23*(3), 244–263. doi: 10.1080/02678370903282600.

Aldwin, C. M., and Revenson, T. A. (1987). Does coping help—A reexamination of the relation between coping and mental-health. *Journal of Personality and Social Psychology, 53*(2), 337–348.

Anderson, C. R. (1977). Locus of control, coping behaviors, and performance in a stress setting: A longitudinal study. *Journal of Applied Psychology, 62*(4), 446–451.

Antonovsky, A. (1984). A call for a new question—salutogenesis—and a proposed answer—the sense of coherence. *Journal of Preventive Psychiatry, 2*(1), 1–11.

———— (1993). The structure and properties of the sense of coherence scale. *Social Science & Medicine, 36*(6), 725–733.

Antonovsky, H., and Sagy, S. (1986). The development of a sense of coherence and its impact on responses to stress situations. *Journal of Social Psychology, 126*(2), 213–225.

Aspinwall, L. G., and Taylor, S. E. (1997). A stitch in time: Self-regulation and proactive coping. *Psychological Bulletin, 121*(3), 417–436.

Austenfeld, J. L., and Stanton, A. L. (2004). Coping through emotional approach: A new look at emotion, coping, and health-related outcomes. *Journal of Personality, 72*(6), 1335–1364. doi: 10.1111/j.1467-6494.2004.00299.x.

Bandura, A. (1982). Self-efficacy mechanism in human agency. *American Psychologist, 37*(2), 122–147.

———— (1989). Regulation of cognitive-processes through perceived self-efficacy. *Developmental Psychology, 25*(5), 729–735.

———— (2006). Guide for constructing self-efficacy scales, *Self-Efficacy Beliefs of Adolescents, 5*, 307–337.

Bandura, A., Cioffi, D., Taylor, C. B., and Brouillard, M. E. (1988). Perceived self-efficacy in coping with cognitive stressors and opioid activation. *Journal of Personality and Social Psychology, 55*(3), 479–488.

Bar-On, R. (2004). "The Bar-On Emotional Quotient Inventory (EQ-i): Rationale, description and summary of psychometric properties."

Bartone, P. T., Roland, R. R., Picano, J. J., and Williams, T. (2008). Psychological hardiness predicts success in US Army Special Forces candidates. *International Journal of Selection and Assessment, 16*(1), 78–81.

Bates, M. J., Bowles, S., Hammermeister, J., Stokes, C., Pinder, E., Moore, M., Fritts, M., Vythilingam, M., Yosick, T., Rhodes, J., Myatt, C., Westphal, R., Fautua, D, Hammer, P., and Burbelo, G. (2010). Psychological fitness. *Military Medicine, 175* (Supplement), 21–38.

Baumeister, R. F., and Heatherton, T. F. (1996). Self-regulation failure: An overview. *Psychological Inquiry, 7*(1), 1–15.

Baumeister, R., Heatherton, T., and Tice, D. (1994). *Losing Control: How and Why People Fail at Self-Regulation.* San Diego: Academic Press.

Baumeister, R. F., Campbell, J. D., Krueger, J. I., and Vohs, K. D. (2003). Does high self-esteem cause better performance, interpersonal success, happiness, or healthier lifestyles? *Psychological Science*, 1–44.

Beaton, R., Murphy, S., Johnson, C., Pike, K., and Corneil, W. (1999). Coping responses and posttraumatic stress symptomatology in urban fire service personnel. *Journal of Traumatic Stress, 12*(2), 293–308.

Beck, K. H. (1980). Development and validation of a dental-health locus of control scale. *Journal of Preventive Dentistry, 6*(5), 327–332.

Benassi, V. A., Sweeney, P. D., and Dufour, C. L. (1988). Is there a relation between locus of control orientation and depression? *Journal of Abnormal Psychology, 97*(3), 357–367.

Bovin, M. J., and Marx, B. P. (2011). The importance of the peritraumatic experience in defining traumatic stress. *Psychological Bulletin, 137*(1), 47–67. doi: 10.1037/a0021353.

Brandon, J. E., Oescher, J., and Loftin, J. M. (1990). The self-control questionnaire: An assessment. *Health Values: Health Behavior, Education & Promotion, 14*(3), 3–9.

Brown, K. W., and Ryan, R. M. (2003). The benefits of being present: Mindfulness and its role in psychological well-being. *Journal of Personality and Social Psychology, 84*(4), 822–848. doi: 10.1037/0022-3514.84.4.822.

Brown, K. W., Ryan, R. A., and Creswell, J. D. (2007). Mindfulness: Theoretical foundations and evidence for its salutary effects. *Psychological Inquiry, 18*(4), 211–237.

Brunwasser, S. M., Gillham, J. E., and Kim, E. S. (2009). A meta-analytic review of the Penn Resiliency Program's effect on depressive symptoms. *Journal of Consulting and Clinical Psychology, 77*(6), 1042–1054. doi: Doi 10.1037/A0017671.

Burton, C. L., Yan, O. H., Pat Horenczyk, R., Chan, I. S. F., Ho, S., and Bonanno, G. A. (2011). Coping flexibility and complicated grief: A comparison of American and Chinese samples. *Depression and Anxiety, 29*, 16–22.

Cacioppo, J. T., Amaral, D. G., Blanchard, J. J., Cameron, J. L., Carter, C. S., Crews, D. (2007). Social neuroscience progress and implications for mental health. *Perspectives on Psychological Science, 2*(2), 99–123. doi: 10.1111/j.1745-6916.2007.00032.x.

Callan, V. J., Terry, D. J., and Schweitzer, R. (1994). Coping resources, coping strategies and adjustment to organizational change: Direct or buffering effects? *Work & Stress, 8*(4), 372–383.

Carmody, J., and Baer, R. A. (2009). How long does a Mmindfulness-based stress reduction program need to be? A review of class contact hours and effect sizes for psychological distress. *Journal of Clinical Psychology, 65*(6), 627–638. doi: 10.1002/Jclp.20555.

Carver, C. S., and Harmon-Jones, E. (2009). Anger is an approach-related affect: Evidence and implications. *Psychological Bulletin, 135*(2), 183–204. doi: 10.1037/a0013965.

Carver, C. S., and Scheier, M. F. (1982). Control theory: A useful conceptual framework for personality-social, clinical, and health psychology. *Psychological Bulletin, 92*(1), 111–135.

Carver, C. S., Scheier, M. F., and Weintraub, J. K. (1989). Assessing coping strategies—A theoretically based approach. *Journal of Personality and Social Psychology, 56*(2), 267–283.

Casey, G. W. (2011). Comprehensive soldier fitness: A vision for psychological resilience in the U.S. Army. *American Psychologist, 66*(1), 1–3. doi: 10.1037/A0021930.

Chang, E. C., Maydeu-Olivares, A., and DZurilla, T. J. (1997). Optimism and pessimism as partially independent constructs: Relationship to positive and negative affectivity and psychological well-being. *Personality and Individual Differences, 23*(3), 433–440.

Chen, G., Thomas, B., and Wallace, J. C. (2005). A multilevel examination of the relationships among training outcomes, mediating regulatory processes, and adaptive performance. *Journal of Applied Psychology, 90*(5), 827–841. doi: 2005-10696-001 [pii] 10.1037/0021-9010.90.5.827.

Cheng, C. (2001). Assessing coping flexibility in real-life and laboratory settings: A multimethod approach. *Journal of Personality and Social Psychology, 80*(5), 814–833. doi: 10.1037//3415.80.5.814.

Chiesa, A., and Serretti, A. (2009). Mindfulness-based stress reduction for stress management in healthy people: A review and meta-analysis. *Journal of Alternative and Complementary Medicine, 15*(5), 593–600. doi: 10.1089/Acm.2008.0495.

Cohen, F., Kearney, K. A., Zegans, L. S., Kemeny, M. E., Neuhaus, J. M., and Stites, D. P. (1999). Differential immune system changes with acute and persistent stress for optimists vs pessimists. *Brain, Behavior, and Immunity, 13*(2), 155–174. doi: 10.1006/brbi.1998.0531S0889-1591(98)90531-1 [pii].

Compas, B. E., Connor-Smith, J. K., Saltzman, H., Thomsen, A. H., and Wadsworth, M. E. (2001). Coping with stress during childhood and adolescence: Problems, progress, and potential in theory and research. *Psychological Bulletin, 127*(1), 87–127. doi: 10.1037/0033-2909.127.1.87.

Connor, K. M., and Davidson, J. R. T. (2003). Development of a new resilience scale: The Connor-Davidson Resilience Scale (CD-RISC). *Depression and Anxiety, 18*(2), 76–82. doi: 10.1002/da.10113.

Connor-Smith, J. K., and Flachsbart, C. (2007). Relations between personality and coping: A meta-analysis. *Journal of Personality and Social Psychology, 93*(6), 1080–1107. doi: 10.1037/0022-3514.93.6.1080.

Cornum, R., Matthews, M. D., and Seligman, M. E. P. (2011). Comprehensive soldier fitness: Building resilience in a challenging institutional context. *American Psychologist, 66*(1), 4–9. doi: 10.1037/A0021420.

DCoE—*See* Defense Centers of Excellence.

Deci, E. L., and Ryan, R. M. (1987). The support of autonomy and the control of behavior. *Journal of Personality and Social Psychology, 53*(6), 1024–1037.

Defense Centers of Excellence for Psychological Health and Traumatic Brain Injury (DCoE). (2011). Traumatic Brain Injury. As of April 9, 2011: http://www.dcoe.health.mil/Content/Navigation/Documents/About%20TBI.pdf

Dember, W. N., and Brooks, J. (1989). A new instrument for measuring optimism and pessimism—Test retest reliability and relations with happiness and religious commitment. *Bulletin of the Psychonomic Society, 27*(4), 365–366.

Dember, W. N., Martin, S. H., Hummer, M. K., Howe, S. R., and Melton, R. S. (1989). The measurement of optimism and pessimism. *Current Psychology-Research & Reviews, 8*(2), 102–119.

Dembinski, R. J. (1979). The reliability of the Self-Control Behavior Inventory. *Behavioral Disorders, 4*(2), 137–142.

Diener, E. (2009). Subjective well-being. In E. Diener (Ed.), *The Science of Well-Being,* Vol. 37, pp. 11–58, Springer Netherlands.

Driskell, J. E., Willis, R. P., and Copper, C. (1992). Effect of overlearning on retention. *Journal of Applied Psychology, 77*(5), 615.

Durlak, J. A., and A. M. Wells (1997). Primary prevention mental health programs for children and adolescents: A meta-analytic review. *American Journal of Community Psychology, 25*(2), 115–152.

Eschleman, K. J., Bowling, N. A., and Alarcon, G. M. (2010). A meta-analytic examination of hardiness. *International Journal of Stress Management, 17*(4), 277.

Fenigstein, A., Scheier, M. F., and Buss, A. H. (1975). Public and private self-consciousness: Assessment and theory. *Journal of Consulting and Clinical Psychology, 43*(4), 522.

Flórez, K. R., Shih, R. A., and Martin, M. T. (forthcoming). *Nutritional Fitness and Resilience: A Review of Relevant Constructs, Measures, and Links to Well-Being.* Santa Monica, Calif.: RAND Corporation, RR-105-AF.

Folkman, S., and Moskowitz, J. T. (2000). Positive affect and the other side of coping. *American Psychologist, 55*(6), 647–654.

Fredrickson, B. L., and Joiner, T. (2002). Positive emotions trigger upward spirals toward emotional well-being. *Psychological Science, 13*(2), 172–175.

Fredrickson, B. L., and Losada, M. F. (2005). Positive affect and the complex dynamics of human flourishing. *American Psychologist, 60*(7), 678–686. doi: 10.1037/0003-066x.60.7.678.

Fredrickson, B. L., Tugade, M. M., Waugh, C. E., and Larkin, G. R. (2003). What good are positive emotions in crises? A prospective study of resilience and emotions following the terrorist attacks on the United States on September 11th, 2001. *Journal of Personality and Social Psychology, 84*(2), 365–376.

Gilbar, O., Ben-Zur, H., and Lubin, G. (2010). Coping, mastery, stress appraisals, mental preparation, and unit cohesion predicting distress and performance: A longitudinal study of soldiers undertaking evacuation tasks. *Anxiety, Stress & Coping, 23*(5), 547–562. doi: 10.1080/10615801003640023.

Greenberg, J., Pyszczynski, T., Burling, J., Simon, L., Solomon, S., Rosenblatt, A., et al. (1992). Why do people need self-esteem—Converging evidence that self-esteem serves an anxiety-buffering function. *Journal of Personality and Social Psychology, 63*(6), 913–922.

Grossman, P., Niemann, L., Schmidt, S., and Walach, H. (2004). Mindfulness-based stress reduction and health benefits—A meta-analysis. *Journal of Psychosomatic Research, 57*(1), 35–43. doi: 10.1016/S0022-3999(03)00573-7.

Haglund, M. E. M., Nestadt, P. S., Cooper, N. S., Southwick, S. M., and Charney, D. S. (2007). Psychobiological mechanisms of resilience: Relevance to prevention and treatment of stress-related psychopathology. *Development and Psychopathology, 19*(03), 889. doi: 10.1017/s0954579407000430.

Harinath, K., Malhotra, A. S., Pal, K., Prasad, R., Kumar, R., Kain, T. C., et al. (2004). Effects of Hatha yoga and Omkar meditation on cardiorespiratory performance, psychologic profile, and melatonin secretion. *Journal of Alternative and Complementary Medicine, 10*(2), 261–268. doi: 10.1089/107555304323062257.

Heatherton, T. F. (2011). Neuroscience of self and self-regulation. *Annual Review of Psychology, Vol 62, 62*, 363–390. doi: 10.1146/annurev.psych.121208.131616.

Hippe, J. (2004). Self-awareness: A precursor to resiliency, *Reclaiming Children and Youth: The Journal of Strength-based Interventions, 12*(4), 240.

Hoge, C. W., Castro, C. A., Messer, S. C., McGurk, D., Cotting, D. I., and Koffman, R. L. (2004). Combat duty in Iraq and Afghanistan, Mental health problems, and barriers to care. *New England Journal of Medicine, 351*(1), 13–22.

Hufford, D. J., Fritts, M. J., and Rhodes, J. E. (2010). Spiritual fitness. *Military Medicine, 175* (Supplement 1), 73–87.

Jackson, B., Sellers, R. M., and Peterson, C. (2002). Pessimistic explanatory style moderates the effect of stress on physical illness. *Personality and Individual Differences, 32*(3), 567–573.

Jha, A. P., Stanley, E. A., Kiyonaga, A., Wong, L., and Gelfand, L. (2010). Examining the protective effects of mindfulness training on working memory capacity and affective experience. *Emotion, 10*(1), 54–64. doi: 10.1037/A0018438.

John, O. P., and Gross, J. J. (2004). Healthy and unhealthy emotion regulation: Personality processes, individual differences, and life span development. *Journal of Personality, 72*(6), 1301–1334. doi: 10.1111/j.1467-6494.2004.00298.x.

Johnson, D. C., Polusny, M. A., Erbes, C. R., King, D., King, L., Litz, B. T., et al. (2011). Development and initial validation of the response to stressful experiences scale. *Military Medicine, 176*(2), 161–169.

Johnson, J. H., and Sarason, I. G. (1978). Life stress, depression and anxiety: Internal-external control as a moderator variable. *Journal of Psychosomatic Research, 22*(3), 205–208. doi: 10.1016/0022-3999(78)90025-9.

Jones, G. R. (1986). Socialization tactics, self-efficacy, and newcomers' adjustments to organizations. *Academy of Management Journal, 29*(2), 262–279.

Judge, T. A., and Bono, J. E. (2001). Relationship of core self-evaluations traits—self-esteem, generalized self-efficacy, locus of control, and emotional stability—with job satisfaction and job performance: A meta-analysis. *Journal of Applied Psychology, 86*(1), 80–92. doi: 10.1037//0021-9010.86.1.80.

Kabat-Zinn, J. (2003). Mindfulness-based interventions in context: Past, present, and future. *Clinical Psychology-Science and Practice, 10*(2), 144–156. doi: 10.1093/Clipsy/Bpg016.

Karoly, P. (1993). Mechanisms of self-regulation—A systems view. *Annual Review of Psychology, 44*, 23–52.

Keyes, C. L. M. (2002). The mental health continuum: From languishing to flourishing in life. *Journal of Health and Social Behavior, 43*(2), 207–222.

Kling, K. C., Hyde, J. S., Showers, C. J., and Buswell, B. N. (1999). Gender differences in self-esteem: A meta-analysis. *Psychological Bulletin, 125*(4), 470–500.

Koenen, K. C. (2006). Developmental epidemiology of PTSD: Self-regulation as a central mechanism. *Annals of the New York Academy of Sciences, 1071*, 255–266. doi: 1071/1/255 [pii] 10.1196/annals.1364.020.

Krause, N., and Stryker, S. (1984). Stress and well-being—The buffering role of locus of control beliefs. *Social Science & Medicine, 18*(9), 783–790.

Lakey, B., Tardiff, T. A., and Drew, J. B. (1994). Negative social interactions—Assessment and relations to social support, cognition, and psychological distress. *Journal of Social and Clinical Psychology, 13*(1), 42–62.

Lakey, C. E., Campbell, W. K., Brown, K. W., and Goodie, A. S. (2007). Dispositional mindfulness as a predictor of the severity of gambling outcomes. *Personality and Individual Differences, 43*(7), 1698–1710. doi: 10.1016/J.Paid.2007.05.007.

Larson, R. (1989). Is feeling in control related to happiness in daily life? *Psychological Reports, 64*(3), 775–784.

Lazarus, R. S., and Folkman, S. (1984). *Stress, Appraisal, and Coping*, New York: Springer Publishing Company.

Leary, M. R., Terdal, S. K., Tambor, E. S., and Downs, D. L. (1995). Self-esteem as an interpersonal monitor—The sociometer hypothesis. *Journal of Personality and Social Psychology, 68*(3), 518–530.

LePine, J. A., Colquitt, J. A., and Erez, A. (2000). Adaptability to changing task contexts: Effects of general cognitive ability conscientiousness, and openness to experience. *Personnel Psychology, 53*(3), 563–593.

Lipsey, M. W., and Wilson, D. B. (1993). The efficacy of psychological, educational, and behavioral treatment—Confirmation from meta-analysis. *American Psychologist, 48*(12), 1181–1209.

Littleton, H., Horsley, S., John, S., and Nelson, D. V. (2007). Trauma coping strategies and psychological distress: A meta-analysis. *Journal of Traumatic Stress, 20*(6), 977–988. doi: 10.1002/jts.20276.

Locke, E. A. (1996). Motivation through conscious goal setting. *Applied and Preventive Psychology, 5*(2), 117–124.

——— (2005). Why emotional intelligence is an invalid concept. *Journal of Organizational Behavior, 26*(4), 425–431. doi: 10.1002/Job.318.

Locke, E. A., and Latham, G. P. (2002). Building a practically useful theory of goal setting and task motivation. *American Psychologist, 57*(9), 705–717.

Luthans, F., Avolio, B. J., Avey, J. B., and Norman, S. M. (2007). Positive psychological capital: Measurement and relationship with performance and satisfaction. *Personnel Psychology, 60*(3), 541–572. doi: 10.1111/J.1744-6570.2007.00083.X.

Lyubomirsky, S., and Della Porta, M. D. (2010). Boosting happiness, buttressing resilience. In J. W. Reich, A. J. Zautra, and J. S. Hall (Eds.), *Handbook of Adult Resilience* (pp. 450–464). New York: The Guilford Press.

Lyubomirsky, S., King, L., and Diener, E. (2005). The benefits of frequent positive affect: Does happiness lead to success? *Psychological Bulletin, 131*(6), 803–855. doi: 10.1037/0033-2909.131.6.803.

Maddi, S. R. (2002). The story of hardiness: Twenty years of theorizing, research, and practice. *Consulting Psychology Journal: Practice and Research, 54*(3), 173.

——— (2005). On hardiness and other pathways to resilience. *American Psychologist, 60*(3), 261–262. doi: 10.1037/0003-066x.60.36.261.

——— (2007). Relevance of hardiness assessment and training to the military context. *Military Psychology, 19*(1), 61–70.

Maes, S., and Karoly, P. (2005). Self-regulation assessment and intervention in physical health and illness: A review. *Applied Psychology-an International Review-Psychologie Appliquee-Revue Internationale, 54*(2), 267–299.

Marks, R., Allegrante, J. P., and Lorig, K. (2005). A review and synthesis of research evidence for self-efficacy-enhancing interventions for reducing chronic disability: Implications for health education practice (part II). *Health Promotion Practice, 6*(2), 148–156. doi: 6/2/148 [pii] 10.1177/1524839904266792.

Martins, A., Ramalho, N., and Morin, E. (2010). A comprehensive meta-analysis of the relationship between emotional intelligence and health. *Personality and Individual Differences, 49*(6), 554–564. doi: 10.1016/J.Paid.2010.05.029.

Maslow, A. H. (1943). A theory of human motivation. *Psychological review, 50*(4), 370.

Mayer, J. D., Salovey, P., and Caruso, D. R. (2008). Emotional intelligence—New ability or eclectic traits? *American Psychologist, 63*(6), 503–517. doi: 10.1037/0003-066x.63.6.503.

McGene, J. (2013). *Social Fitness and Resilience: A Review of Relevant Constructs, Measures, and Links to Well-Being.* Santa Monica, Calif.: RAND Corporation, RR-108-AF. As of October 3, 2013:
http://www.rand.org/pubs/research_reports/RR108.html

Meadows, S. O., and Miller, L. L. (forthcoming). *Airman and Family Resilience: Lessons from the Scientific Literature.* Santa Monica, Calif.: RAND Corporation, RR-106-AF.

Meichenbaum, D. (1985). *Stress Inoculation Training.* New York: Pergamon Press.

Meredith, L. S., Sherbourne, C. D., Gaillot, S., Hansell, L., Ritschard, H. V., Parker, A. M., and Wrenn, G. (2011). *Promoting Psychological Resilience in the U.S. Military.* Santa Monica, Calif.: RAND Corporation, MG-996-OSD. As of May 13, 2013:
http://www.rand.org/pubs/monographs/MG996.html

Morgan, B. J., and Bibb, S. C. G. (2011). Assessment of military population-based psychological resilience programs. *Military Medicine, 176*(9), 976–985.

Morrison, G. M., and Cosden, M. A. (1997). Risk, resilience, and adjustment of individuals with learning disabilities. *Learning Disability Quarterly, 20*(1), 43–60.

Mullen, Admiral M. (2010). On total force fitness in war and peace, *Military Medicine, 175* (Supplement), 1–2.

Multon, K. D., Brown, S. D., and Lent, R. W. (1991). Relation of self-efficacy beliefs to academic outcomes—A meta-analytic investigation. *Journal of Counseling Psychology, 38*(1), 30–38.

Muraven, M., and Baumeister, R. F. (2000). Self-regulation and depletion of limited resources: Does self-control resemble a muscle? *Psychological Bulletin, 126*(2), 247–259.

Nes, L. S., and Segerstrom, S. C. (2006). Dispositional optimism and coping: A meta-analytic review. *Personality and Social Psychology Review, 10*(3), 235–251. doi: 10.1207/s15327957pspr1003_3.

Newcomb, M. D., and Harlow, L. L. (1986). Life events and substance use among adolescents: Mediating effects of perceived loss of control and meaninglessness in life. *Journal of Personality and Social Psychology, 51*(3), 564–577. doi: 10.1037/0022-3514.51.3.564.

Ng, T. W. H., Sorensen, K. L., and Eby, L. T. (2006). Locus of control at work: A meta-analysis. *Journal of Organizational Behavior, 27*(8), 1057–1087. doi: 10.1002/job.416.

O'Connor, P., Campbell, J., Newon, J., Melton, J., Salas, E., and Wilson, K. A. (2008). Crew resource management training effectiveness: A meta-analysis and some critical needs. *The International Journal of Aviation Psychology, 18*(4), 353–368.

Orasanu, J. M., and Backer, P. (1996). Stress and military performance. In J. E. Driskell and E. Salas (Eds.), *Stress and Human Performance* (pp. 89–126). Mahwah, N.J.: Lawrence Erlbaum Associates.

Pearlin, L. I., and Schooler, C. (1978). The structure of coping. *Journal of Health and Social Behavior*, 2–21.

Penley, J. A., Tomaka, J., and Wiebe, J. S. (2002). The association of coping to physical and psychological health outcomes: A meta-analytic review. *Journal of Behavioral Medicine, 25*(6), 551–603.

Peterson, C. (1991). The meaning and measurement of Eexplanatory style. *Psychological Inquiry, 2*(1), 1–10.

Peterson, C., Seligman, M. E., and Vaillant, G. E. (1988). Pessimistic explanatory style is a risk factor for physical illness: A thirty-five-year longitudinal study. *Journal of Personality and Social Psychology, 55*(1), 23–27.

Peterson, C., Semmel, A., Vonbaeyer, C., Abramson, L. Y., Metalsky, G. I., and Seligman, M. E. P. (1982). The attributional style questionnaire. *Cognitive Therapy and Research, 6*(3), 287–299.

Posner, M. I., and Rothbart, M. K. (2000). Developing mechanisms of self-regulation. *Development and Psychopathology, 12*(3), 427–441.

Prati, G., and Pietrantoni, L. (2009). Optimism, social support, and coping strategies as factors contributing to posttraumatic growth: A meta-analysis. *Journal of Loss and Trauma, 14*(5), 364–388. doi: 10.1080/15325020902724271.

Pulakos, E. D., Arad, S., Donovan, M. A., and Plamondon, K. E. (2000). Adaptability in the workplace: Development of a taxonomy of adaptive performance. *Journal of Applied Psychology, 85*(4), 612–624. doi: 10.1037//0021-9010.85.4.612.

42

Pyszczynski, T., Solomon, S., Greenberg, J., Arndt, J., and Schimel, J. (2004). Why do people need self-esteem? A theoretical and empirical review. *Psychological Bulletin, 130*(3), 435–468. doi: 10.1037/0033-2909.130.3.435.

Ramchand, R. N., Acosta, J., Burns, R. M., Jaycox, L., and Pernin, C. G. (2011). *The War Within: Preventing Suicide in the U.S. Military.* Santa Monica, Calif.: RAND Corporation, MG-953-OSD. As of May 13, 2013:
http://www.rand.org/pubs/monographs/MG953.html

Rasmussen, H. N., Scheier, M. F., and Greenhouse, J. B. (2009). Optimism and physical health: A meta-analytic review. *Annals of Behavioral Medicine, 37*(3), 239–256. doi: 10.1007/s12160-009-9111-x.

Reis, H. T., Sheldon, K. M., Gable, S. L., Roscoe, J., and Ryan, R. M. (2000). Daily well-being: The role of autonomy, competence, and relatedness. *Personality and Social Psychology Bulletin, 26*(4), 419–435. doi: 10.1177/0146167200266002.

Reivich, K. J., Seligman, M. E. P., and McBride, S. (2011). Master resilience training in the US Army. *American Psychologist, 66*(1), 25–34. doi: 10.1037/A0021897.

Richardson, G. E. (2002). The metatheory of resilience and resiliency. *Journal of Clinical Psychology, 58*(3), 307–321. doi: 10.1002/Jclp.10020.

Richardson, K. M., and Rothstein, H. R. (2008). Effects of occupational stress management intervention programs: A meta-analysis. *Journal of Occupational Health Psychology, 13*(1), 69–93. doi: 10.1037/1076-8998.13.1.69.

Richeson, J. A., and Shelton, J. N. (2003). When prejudice does not pay: Effects of interracial contact on executive function. *Psychological Science, 14*(3), 287–290.

Robins, R. W., Hendin, H. M., and Trzesniewski, K. H. (2001). Measuring global self-esteem: Construct validation of a single-item measure and the Rosenberg self-esteem scale. *Personality and Social Psychology Bulletin, 27*(2), 151–161. doi: 10.1177/0146167201272002.

Robson, S. (2013). *Physical Fitness and Resilience: A Review of Relevant Constructs, Measures, and Links to Well-Being.* Santa Monica, Calif.: RAND Corporation, RR-104-AF. As of October 3, 2013:
http://www.rand.org/pubs/research_reports/RR104.html

——— (2014). *Psychological Fitness and Resilience: A Review of Relevant Constructs, Measures, and Links to Well-Being.* Santa Monica, Calif.: RAND Corporation, RR-102-AF. As of March 2014:
http://www.rand.org/pubs/research_reports/RR102.html

Robson, S., and Salcedo, N. (forthcoming). *Behavioral Fitness and Resilience: A Review of Relevant Constructs, Measures, and Links to Well-Being.* Santa Monica, Calif.: RAND Corporation, RR-103-AF.

Rodrigues, C. S., and Renshaw, K. D. (2010). Associations of coping processes with posttraumatic stress disorder symptoms in national guard/reserve service members deployed during the OEF-OIF era. *Journal of Anxiety Disorders, 24*(7), 694–699. doi: 10.1016/j.janxdis.2010.04.013.

Rosen, M. A., Bedwell, W. L., Wildman, J. L., Fritzsche, B. A., Salas, E., and Burke, C. S. (2011). Managing adaptive performance in teams: Guiding principles and behavioral markers for measurement. *Human Resource Management Review, 21*(2), 107–122. doi: 10.1016/J.Hrmr.2010.09.003.

Rosenbaum, M. (1980). Schedule for assessing self-control behaviors—Preliminary findings. *Behavior Therapy, 11*(1), 109–121.

Rosenberg, M. (1965). *Society and the Adolescent Self-Image.* Princeton, N.J.: Princeton University Press.

Roth, S., and Cohen, L. J. (1986). Approach, avoidance, and coping with stress. *American Psychologist, 41*(7), 813–819. doi: 10.1037//0003-066x.41.7.813.

Rotter, J. B. (1966). Generalized expectancies for internal versus external control of reinforcement. *Psychological Monographs: General & Applied, 80*(1), 1–28.

Rutter, M. (1985). Resilience in the face of adversity—Protective factors and resistance to psychiatric-disorder. *British Journal of Psychiatry, 147*, 598–611.

Ryff, C. D. (1989). Happiness is everything, or is it—Explorations on the meaning of psychological well-being. *Journal of Personality and Social Psychology, 57*(6), 1069–1081.

Salas, E., Burke, C. S., Bowers, C. A., and Wilson, K. A. (2001). Team training in the skies: Does crew resource management (CRM) training work? *Human Factors: The Journal of the Human Factors and Ergonomics Society, 43*(4), 641.

Salovey, P., and J. D. Mayer (1990). Emotional intelligence: Imagination, cognition, and personality, *Emotional Intelligence: Key Readings in the Mayer and Salovey Model*, 185–211.

Saunders, T., Driskell, J. E., Johnston, J. H., and Salas, E. (1996). The effect of stress inoculation training on anxiety and performance. *Journal of Occupational Health Psychology, 1*(2), 170–186.

Scheier, M. F., and Carver, C. S. (1985). Optimism, coping, and health—Assessment and implications of generalized outcome expectancies. *Health Psychology, 4*(3), 219–247.

Schutte, N. S., Malouff, J. M., Thorsteinsson, E. B., Bhullar, N., and Rooke, S. E. (2007). A meta-analytic investigation of the relationship between emotional intelligence and health. *Personality and Individual Differences, 42*(6), 921–933. doi: 10.1016/ J.Paid.2006.09.003.

Segerstrom, S. C. (2005). Optimism and immunity: Do positive thoughts always lead to positive effects? *Brain, Behavior, and Immunity, 19*(3), 195–200. doi: S0889-1591(04)00120-5 [pii] 10.1016/j.bbi.2004.08.003.

Seligman, M. E. P. (2002). *Authentic Happiness: Using the New Positive Psychology to Realize Your Potential for Lasting Fulfillment.* New York: Free Press.

———— (2011a). *Learned Optimism: How to Change Your Mind and Your Life.* New York: Vintage.

———— (2011b). Building resilience. *Harvard Business Review, 89*(4), 100+.

Seligman, M. E. P., and Fowler, R. D. (2011). Comprehensive soldier fitness and the future of psychology. *American Psychologist, 66*(1), 82–86. doi: 10.1037/A0021898.

Seligman, M. E. P., Rashid, T., and Parks, A. C. (2006). Positive psychotherapy. *American Psychologist, 61*(8), 774.

Seligman, M. E. P., Steen, T. A., Park, N., and Peterson, C. (2005). Positive psychology progress: Empirical validation of interventions. *American Psychologist, 60*(5), 410–421.

Shih, R. A., Meadows, S. O., and Martin, M. T. (2013). *Medical Fitness and Resilience: A Review of Relevant Constructs, Measures, and Links to Well-Being.* Santa Monica, Calif.: RAND Corporation, RR-107-AF. As of October 3, 2013: http://www.rand.org/pubs/research_reports/RR107.html

Shih, R. A., Meadows, S. O., Mendeloff, J., and Bowling, K. (forthcoming). *Environmental Fitness and Resilience: A Review of Relevant Constructs, Measures, and Links to Well-Being.* Santa Monica, Calif.: RAND Corporation, RR-101-AF.

Shilts, M. K., Horowitz, M., and Townsend, M. S. (2004). Goal setting as a strategy for dietary and physical activity behavior change: A review of the literature. *American Journal of Health Promotion, 19*, 81–93.

Sieber, W. J., Rodin, J., Larson, L., Ortega, S., Cummings, N., Levy, S., et al. (1992). Modulation of human natural killer cell activity by exposure to uncontrollable stress. *Brain Behavior and Immununity, 6*(2), 141–156. doi: 0889-1591(92)90014-F [pii].

Sin, N. L., and Lyubomirsky, S. (2009). Enhancing well-being and alleviating depressive symptoms with positive psychology interventions: A practice-friendly meta-analysis. *Journal of Clinical Psychology, 65*(5), 467–487. doi: 10.1002/Jclp.20593.

Skinner, E. A., Edge, K., Altman, J., and Sherwood, H. (2003). Searching for the structure of coping: A review and critique of category systems for classifying ways of coping. *Psychological Bulletin, 129*(2), 216–269. doi: 10.1037/0033-2909.129.2.216.

Skomorovsky, A., and Sudom, K. A. (2011). Role of hardiness in the psychological well-being of Canadian forces officer candidates. *Military Medicine, 176*(1), 7–12.

Solomon, Z., Mikulincer, M., and Avitzur, E. (1988). Coping, locus of control, social support, and combat-related posttraumatic stress disorder: A prospective study. *Journal of Personality and Social Psychology, 55*(2), 279–285. doi: 10.1037/0022-3514.55.2.279.

Solomon, Z., Mikulincer, M., and Flum, H. (1988). Negative life events, coping responses, and combat-related psychopathology—A prospective-study. *Journal of Abnormal Psychology, 97*(3), 302–307.

Spector, P. E. (1988). Development of the work locus of control scale. *Journal of Occupational Psychology, 61*(4), 335–340.

Stajkovic, A. D., and Luthans, F. (1998). Self-efficacy and work-related performance: A meta-analysis. *Psychological Bulletin, 124*(2), 240–261.

Stanton, A. L., Danoff-Burg, S., Cameron, C. L., and Ellis, A. P. (1994). Coping through emotional approach: Problems of conceptualizaton and confounding. *Journal of Personality and Social Psychology, 66*(2), 350.

Steele, C. M., Spencer, S. J., and Lynch, M. (1993). Self-image resilience and dissonance: The role of affirmational resources. *Journal of Personality and Social Psychology, 64*(6), 885–896.

Sweeney, P. D., Anderson, K., and Bailey, S. (1986). Attributional style in depression—A meta-analytic review. *Journal of Personality and Social Psychology, 50*(5), 974–991.

Tangney, J. P., Baumeister, R. F., and Boone, A. L. (2004). High self-control predicts good adjustment, less pathology, better grades, and interpersonal success. *Journal of Personality, 72*(2), 271–324.

Tanielian, T. L., Jaycox, L., Adamson, D. M., Burnam, M. A., Burns, R. M., Caldarone, L. B., et al.(2008). *Invisible Wounds of War: Psychological and Cognitive Injuries, Their Consequences, and Services to Assist Recovery*. Santa Monica, Calif.: RAND Corporation, MG-720-CCF. As of May 13, 2013: http://www.rand.org/pubs/monographs/MG720.html.

Taylor, M. K., Mujica-Parodi, L. R., Padilla, G. A., Markham, A. E., Potterat, E. G., Momen, N., et al. (2009). Behavioral predictors of acute stress symptoms during intense military training. *Journal of Traumatic Stress, 22*(3), 212–217. doi: 10.1002/ jts.20413.

Taylor, S. E., Kemeny, M. E., Reed, G. M., Bower, J. E., and Gruenewald, T. L. (2000). Psychological resources, positive illusions, and health. *American Psychologist, 55*(1), 99–109.

Trapnell, P. D., and Campbell, J. D. (1999). Private self-consciousness and the five-factor model of personality: Distinguishing rumination from reflection. *Journal of Personality and Social Psychology, 76*(2), 284–304.

Tugade, M. M., and Fredrickson, B. L. (2004). Resilient individuals use positive emotions to bounce back from negative emotional experiences. *Journal of Personality and Social Psychology, 86*(2), 320–333. doi: 10.1037/0022-3514.86.2.3202004-10747-009 [pii].

Vogt, D. S., Rizvi, S. L., Shipherd, J. C., and Resick, P. A. (2008). Longitudinal investigation of reciprocal relationship between stress reactions and hardiness. *Personality and Social Psychology Bulletin, 34*(1), 61–73. doi: 10.1177/ 0146167207309197.

Walach, H., Buchheld, N., Buttenm̦ller, V., Kleinknecht, N., and Schmidt, S. (2006). Measuring mindfulness—The Freiburg Mindfulness Inventory (FMI). *Personality and Individual Differences, 40*(8), 1543–1555.

Watson, D., Clark, L. A., and Tellegen, A. (1988). Development and validation of brief measures of positive and negative affect: The PANAS scales. *Journal of Personality and Social Psychology, 54*(6), 1063–1070.

Wiedenfeld, S. A., Bandura, A., Levine, S., Oleary, A., Brown, S., and Raska, K. (1990). Impact of perceived self-efficacy in coping with stressors on components of the immune-system. *Journal of Personality and Social Psychology, 59*(5), 1082–1094.

Winefield, H. R. (1982). Reliability and validity of the health locus of control scale. *Journal of Personality Assessment, 46*(6), 614–619.

Wood, W. D., and Letak, J. K. (1982). A mental-health locus of control scale. *Personality and Individual Differences, 3*(1), 84–87.

Yeung, D., and Martin, M. T. (2013). *Spiritual Fitness and Resilience: A Review of Relevant Constructs, Measures, and Links to Well-Being.* Santa Monica, Calif.: RAND Corporation, RR-100-AF. As of October 3, 2013:
http://www.rand.org/pubs/research_reports/RR100.html

Youssef, C. M., and Luthans, F. (2007). Positive organizational behavior in the workplace: The impact of hope, optimism, and resilience. *Journal of Management, 33*(5), 774–800. doi: 10.1177/0149206307305562.